THE TEACHER OF RIGHTEOUSNESS AND THE WICKED PRIEST

THEIR ROLES, RIVALRY, CONFLICT, AND DIVINE JUDGMENT IN THE DEAD SEA SCROLLS

EDWARD D. ANDREWS

THE TEACHER OF RIGHTEOUSNESS AND THE WICKED PRIEST

Their Roles, Rivalry, Conflict, and Divine Judgment in the Dead Sea Scrolls

Edward D. Andrews

Christian Publishing House

Cambridge, Ohio

THE TEACHER OF RIGHTEOUSNESS AND THE WICKED PRIEST: Their Roles, Rivalry, Conflict, and Divine Judgment in the Dead Sea Scrolls by Edward D. Andrews

ISBN-13: 9798344462066

Table of Contents

Preface

The Dead Sea Scrolls have shed light on an ancient community's fervent pursuit of righteousness amidst a turbulent era in Jewish history. Central to these texts are two enigmatic figures whose lives and beliefs embody the intense spiritual and ideological conflicts of the Second Temple period: the Teacher of Righteousness and the Wicked Priest. Together, these two adversaries represent the opposing forces within a divided religious landscape, providing insights into a time when questions of purity, covenant, and divine judgment defined the lives of those who longed for Jehovah's favor.

The Teacher of Righteousness, revered by his followers in the Qumran community, is portrayed as a visionary leader and interpreter of God's law. To his community, he was a beacon of truth, guiding them toward a higher moral and spiritual standard. His commitment to living in strict obedience to Jehovah's commandments inspired a way of life that set the Qumran community apart from mainstream Judaism. In contrast, the Wicked Priest appears as the Teacher's bitter adversary—a figure associated with corruption, moral decay, and, allegedly, the desecration of the Temple. This conflict, documented in several Dead Sea Scrolls, paints a vivid picture of the struggles between those who sought to honor the covenant with Jehovah and those accused of straying from it.

In writing this book, *The Teacher of Righteousness and the Wicked Priest,* we seek to unravel the mystery surrounding these two figures. The book delves deeply into the scrolls that mention them, exploring the historical, religious, and theological contexts that gave rise to this intense rivalry. It considers the Teacher's teachings on righteousness and covenant, his role as a prophetic leader, and his eschatological vision of divine justice. In turn, it examines the Wicked Priest's role as a symbol of apostasy and religious compromise, and the Qumran community's belief that divine judgment awaited him.

The Teacher of Righteousness and the Wicked Priest are more than historical figures; they are enduring symbols of the battle between truth and corruption, loyalty to Jehovah and the lure of secular power. Their lives prompt us to reflect on the nature of true faith, the cost of standing for righteousness, and the dangers of spiritual compromise. These themes resonate beyond the boundaries of time and culture, offering profound lessons for those who seek to understand the timeless struggle between light and darkness, obedience and rebellion.

In this book, we aim to provide a thorough study of these two figures and the spiritual dynamics that shaped the Qumran community. This journey takes us into the heart of ancient Jewish thought, exploring the beliefs and aspirations of a people deeply devoted to the pursuit of divine truth. May this exploration encourage readers to reflect on the importance of remaining steadfast in faith and undivided in loyalty to the God who judges all with righteousness.

Edward D. Andrews

Author of 220+ books and Chief Translator of the Updated American Standard Version (UASV)

Edward D. Andrews

Introduction

In the vast landscape of Second Temple Judaism, the Qumran community stands out as one of the most unique and enigmatic groups of the period. The discovery of the Dead Sea Scrolls—arguably one of the greatest archaeological finds of the 20th century—has granted scholars and believers alike a window into this community's spiritual life, values, and struggles. Within these ancient texts, we find a community committed to a distinct way of life, rooted in what they perceived as a divine calling to preserve the purity of their covenant with Jehovah. Central to their worldview were two figures whose lives and teachings encapsulate the community's theological and ideological framework: the Teacher of Righteousness and the Wicked Priest.

The Teacher of Righteousness emerges in the scrolls as a revered leader, whose interpretation of the Scriptures and passion for righteousness guided the community in their isolation. Unlike other Jewish groups of the time, the Qumran sect saw itself as an "elect" community, bound by a special relationship with Jehovah and set apart from what they viewed as a corrupted mainstream religious establishment. To the members of this community, the Teacher of Righteousness was more than a mere leader; he was a prophet and moral authority who illuminated the path of righteousness amid a darkened world. Through his teachings, he provided his followers with both guidance and reassurance, offering them a theological framework to understand their role in the unfolding of divine history.

Standing in stark contrast to the Teacher is the figure of the Wicked Priest, a personage vilified in the scrolls as one who compromised the covenant and symbolized spiritual corruption. Representing everything that the Qumran community rejected, the Wicked Priest is depicted as a religious leader who wielded power irresponsibly and disregarded the sanctity of the Temple and the law. For the Teacher and his followers, the Wicked Priest was more than just a theological adversary; he embodied the spiritual decline of the religious establishment, a symbol of the dangers of deviating from Jehovah's ways. This rivalry between the Teacher and the Wicked Priest underscores a broader clash within Jewish society—a battle between those devoted to divine law and those who, in the Qumran community's eyes, had lost their way.

In this book, we embark on a journey to understand the Qumran community's worldview through the lens of this rivalry. What drove these men to live such radically different lives, and how did their actions shape the beliefs of those around them? This exploration involves an in-depth examination of the Dead Sea Scrolls, particularly texts like the *Damascus Document, The Community Rule*, and *The Habakkuk Commentary*, which mention the Teacher of Righteousness and his confrontations with the Wicked Priest. Through these texts, we gain insight not only into the figures themselves but into the deeply held convictions of the Qumran community—convictions that led them to separate themselves from the broader Jewish population and to view themselves as the true faithful remnant of Jehovah.

This study does not simply present a historical analysis but seeks to grasp the underlying theological questions that drove these figures and their followers. Why did the Qumran community believe that isolation was necessary for spiritual purity? What role did prophecy and interpretation of Scripture play in defining their identity? And perhaps most importantly, how did their intense eschatological expectations shape their perception of both the Teacher of Righteousness and the Wicked Priest?

By understanding these questions, we can better appreciate the significance of the Teacher of Righteousness and the Wicked Priest beyond the Qumran community. These figures embody timeless themes: the struggle for purity in worship, the dangers of compromising faith for power, and the hope that Jehovah will ultimately judge righteously. In following this narrative, we hope not only to uncover the historical realities of these figures but also to reflect on the spiritual lessons their lives offer to modern readers.

Through a careful examination of the Dead Sea Scrolls and the contexts surrounding these two figures, *The Teacher of Righteousness and the Wicked Priest* aims to paint a full picture of this rivalry that shaped an entire community's beliefs and practices. We invite readers to delve into this world of fervent devotion and ideological conflict, discovering what drove these men and how their lives continue to resonate with those who seek to follow the path of righteousness in a world filled with spiritual challenges.

SECTION 1 The Teacher of Righteousness: Unveiling the Enigmatic Figure of the Dead Sea Scrolls

CHAPTER 1 Introduction: The Mystery of the Teacher of Righteousness

The discovery of the Dead Sea Scrolls has opened an unparalleled window into the world of the Qumran community—a group of Jewish sectarians who thrived in a period of profound religious and political turmoil in the centuries leading up to and including the lifetime of Jesus. These scrolls contain invaluable religious texts, including mentions of two enigmatic figures: the Teacher of Righteousness and the Wicked Priest. The Teacher of Righteousness, revered and followed by this isolated community, emerges in the scrolls as a profound spiritual and moral leader whose teachings shaped the identity, beliefs, and practices of this group. But who was this Teacher? What is the origin of his influence and authority, and how did his role shape the contours of faith within the Qumran sect?

The title "Teacher of Righteousness" is unique within the literature of the Dead Sea Scrolls and is used to denote someone set apart for his unique interpretation and understanding of God's law. His life and ministry offer us insight into the theological framework, aspirations, and eschatological hopes of a sect deeply committed to holiness, separation from mainstream religious practices, and loyalty to Jehovah's covenant. In exploring the significance of this Teacher, we encounter a figure who not only sought purity and covenantal faithfulness but who also became a focal point of opposition to a corrupted priesthood.

The Identity and Role of the Teacher of Righteousness

Within the Dead Sea Scrolls, the Teacher of Righteousness is never explicitly named. This absence of identification has led to significant scholarly debate, but the scrolls themselves provide sufficient context to form a portrait of the Teacher's character and significance. The Teacher of Righteousness is described as a prophetic leader and interpreter of God's law, a man who seemed to emerge during a time of national crisis and led his community to uphold what he deemed to be the true form of worship. His authority rested not on political power or temple priesthood lineage but on his profound understanding of Scripture and his role as a divinely appointed guide to righteousness.

One of the key texts that introduce the Teacher of Righteousness is the *Damascus Document*, a manuscript detailing aspects of the community's covenantal beliefs, codes of conduct, and warnings against apostasy. Here, the Teacher is portrayed as a man of unique insight and devotion, chosen by Jehovah to illuminate the true path of righteousness. According to the community's beliefs, he received divine revelation to interpret and apply the Law of Moses in a time when many felt that the religious leadership had strayed from God's commandments.

This emphasis on the Teacher's unique authority suggests a leader who, like the prophets of old, was seen as divinely inspired to call others back to covenant faithfulness. However, his focus on interpreting God's law diverged sharply from the mainstream religious leaders of the time, who held considerable power within the temple and were seen by the Qumran sect as having abandoned the true spirit of the Mosaic covenant. This divergence created a significant rift between the Teacher of Righteousness and the established priestly class, embodied in the figure of the Wicked Priest. This title, the Wicked Priest, likely refers to a high priest who was seen as corrupt and compromised, contributing to the moral and spiritual decay that the Qumran community vehemently opposed.

The Authority of the Teacher of Righteousness: A Prophet, Priest, and Interpreter

The Teacher of Righteousness functioned as a prophet for the Qumran community, declaring that his guidance came directly from Jehovah. His prophetic authority is reminiscent of figures such as Moses, Samuel, and the Old Testament prophets, who were divinely called to lead the people back to faithfulness. The Teacher's teachings included interpretations of Scriptural prophecies and insights, demonstrating a profound command of the Hebrew Scriptures and aligning himself with a prophetic tradition that often stood in opposition to corrupted religious leaders.

The *Habakkuk Commentary* found among the scrolls provides an example of the Teacher's role in offering interpretation. In his interpretation of Habakkuk's prophecies, the Teacher applied the Scriptures to his own time, suggesting that the conflicts and judgments foretold by the prophet were unfolding in their own day. This interpretive method reveals the Teacher's theological framework: he believed that Scriptural prophecy was not only relevant to the ancient Israelites but continued to speak to Jehovah's people across generations. His interpretations were viewed as revelatory and central to guiding the community's religious practices.

A Life Set Apart: Holiness and Covenant in the Teacher's Teaching

The teachings of the Teacher of Righteousness placed great emphasis on purity, righteousness, and obedience to Jehovah's covenant. The Qumran community, under his leadership, saw itself as the true remnant of Israel, distinct from the corrupted practices of mainstream Judaism. This separatist stance did not arise from mere preference but rather from a deep conviction that they alone represented God's faithful covenant people. In this regard, the Teacher's role was not only to interpret the law but to embody it, serving as a model of holiness and commitment to God's commandments.

One prominent theme in the Teacher's teachings is the covenant—an enduring agreement between Jehovah and His people. The Qumran community's identity was deeply rooted in this covenantal relationship, which they believed to be upheld through strict observance of the Mosaic Law. In this respect, the Teacher of Righteousness emphasized a kind of holiness that went beyond mere ritual, focusing instead on ethical and moral purity. This echoes the sentiments found in Deuteronomy, where the nation of Israel is repeatedly called to "be holy, for I, Jehovah your God, am holy" (Leviticus 19:2). The Teacher's instructions to his followers were thus aligned with the Torah's call to covenant faithfulness and separation from corruption.

The Teacher's interpretation of the Law likely included aspects of both ritual and ethical purity. Ritual purity involved adherence to specific laws concerning cleanliness, dietary restrictions, and observances, whereas ethical purity focused on righteousness in behavior and intentions. This dual emphasis aligns with the Torah's teachings, underscoring the holistic nature of obedience that the Teacher promoted. According to the Qumran community's writings, the Teacher called his followers to a standard of righteousness that set them apart not only from Gentiles but from other Jews who had deviated from the strict path.

Eschatological Beliefs and Divine Judgment in the Teacher's Message

One of the most defining aspects of the Teacher's role was his focus on eschatology, or the study of end times. The Qumran community, shaped by the Teacher's teachings, believed they were living in the "last days" and awaited Jehovah's imminent judgment on a sinful world. This belief in an approaching divine intervention was central to their worldview and is reflected in the apocalyptic tone of many of their writings.

The Teacher's eschatological message was likely influenced by the prophecies of the Hebrew Bible, particularly the writings of prophets like Isaiah, Jeremiah, and Ezekiel, who foretold judgment and restoration. In the Teacher's view, the Qumran community was the righteous remnant through whom Jehovah would establish His kingdom on earth. The scrolls frequently express a hope for divine vengeance upon the wicked and restoration for the faithful. Passages like Isaiah 66:15-16, which describe Jehovah's coming in fire to "render his anger in fury, and his rebuke with flames of fire," would have resonated strongly with the community's belief that their isolation and righteousness would ultimately be vindicated by divine judgment.

The eschatological teachings of the Teacher also underscore the community's separation from mainstream Jewish society, which they regarded as corrupt and condemned. The belief that Jehovah's judgment was soon to come motivated the community to maintain a rigorous standard of holiness, as they prepared for the coming "day of Jehovah," a concept echoed in passages like Joel 2:1, which warns, "Let all the inhabitants of the land tremble, for the day of Jehovah is coming; it is near." This apocalyptic outlook reinforced their identity as the chosen remnant and justified their rejection of mainstream religious practices that they deemed compromised or impure.

Conflict with the Wicked Priest: Opposition from a Corrupted Religious Leader

The figure of the Wicked Priest represents the opposition to the Teacher of Righteousness and embodies what the Qumran community saw as the moral and spiritual decay of the established priesthood. Although the identity of the Wicked Priest is not definitively known, the Dead Sea Scrolls describe him as a priestly figure who abandoned the true path and led others astray. This conflict between the Teacher and the Wicked Priest illustrates a significant divide within Jewish society of the time, with one group devoted to purity and covenant faithfulness and the other accused of defilement and apostasy.

According to the scrolls, the Wicked Priest pursued the Teacher and sought to undermine his influence, possibly even attempting to harm him physically. This hostility was seen as evidence of the priesthood's corruption, with the Teacher and his followers viewing themselves as a persecuted minority defending true faith. The conflict with the Wicked Priest underscores the Qumran community's disdain for the established priestly authorities, whom they believed had forsaken the covenant for personal gain and power.

The Teacher of Righteousness: Legacy of Faithfulness to Jehovah's Covenant

The Teacher of Righteousness, through his teachings and life, left a profound impact on the Qumran community, shaping its values and aspirations for generations. His role as a leader who emphasized the centrality of Jehovah's covenant and the need for holiness resonated deeply with his followers. They viewed him not as an abstract religious figure but as a living embodiment of faithfulness in a time of widespread corruption. In his emphasis on purity, covenant, and divine judgment, the Teacher represented a continuity with the prophets of old while also bringing a unique interpretation that addressed the specific challenges faced by his community.

The community's writings express a conviction that, through their adherence to the Teacher's message, they would receive divine favor and protection in the time of judgment. The Teacher's focus on righteousness as the path to salvation is echoed in passages such as Isaiah 26:2-3, which declares, "Open the gates, that the righteous nation that keeps faith may enter in. You keep him in perfect peace whose mind is stayed on you because he trusts in you." For the Qumran sect, the Teacher's teachings were not just guidance but a divine mandate that provided the assurance of Jehovah's approval.

In understanding the Teacher of Righteousness, we gain insight into the motivations and beliefs that defined the Qumran community. His life and ministry offer a powerful example of commitment to Jehovah's covenant amid a period of crisis, and his legacy serves as a reminder of the ongoing struggle between faithfulness and compromise. As we explore the scrolls further, the figure of the Teacher of Righteousness emerges not only as a historical leader but as a symbol of the enduring call to righteousness.

CHAPTER 2 The Discovery of the Dead Sea Scrolls

Introduction to the Discovery of the Dead Sea Scrolls: A Historical Turning Point

The discovery of the Dead Sea Scrolls is a monumental event in the study of ancient religious texts, shedding light on the beliefs and practices of a secluded Jewish community and offering insights into the broader context of Jewish faith and thought in the Second Temple period. In early 1947, a young Bedouin shepherd inadvertently stumbled upon one of the most significant archaeological finds of the 20th century in the remote Judean desert near the Dead Sea, just northeast of Jerusalem. The scrolls he discovered were stored in clay jars within caves, untouched for centuries, and they contained texts that had been preserved through a remarkable combination of the arid desert climate and careful storage.

The writings found within these scrolls are attributed to a group that likely separated from mainstream Jewish practices due to disagreements over religious purity and covenantal loyalty. Known today as the Qumran community, this sect dedicated itself to a lifestyle that, in their view, upheld the true Mosaic covenant as commanded by Jehovah. The scrolls unearthed at Qumran provide invaluable perspectives on this group's theological views, their interpretation of the Hebrew Scriptures, and their strict adherence to a distinctive religious lifestyle.

What Are the Dead Sea Scrolls? Texts That Illuminate Early Jewish Thought

The Dead Sea Scrolls include a wide variety of writings, from sectarian documents unique to the Qumran community to copies of canonical and non-canonical Hebrew texts. Among these scrolls are fragments from nearly every book of the Hebrew Bible, dating as far back as the third century B.C.E., with the exceptions of the Book of Esther. Some texts appear to be earlier versions of what later became the accepted Hebrew Scriptures, while others reflect unique interpretations of those Scriptures.

These texts are divided into three primary categories: Biblical manuscripts, sectarian writings, and other literature.

Biblical Manuscripts: Earliest Copies of Scripture

The Biblical manuscripts discovered among the Dead Sea Scrolls include fragments of almost every book of the Hebrew Bible, providing the earliest known copies of these texts and offering crucial evidence for the textual reliability of the Scriptures. These manuscripts predate the Masoretic Text, which became the authoritative version of the Hebrew Bible, by roughly a thousand years.

Some of the most complete scrolls include the Great Isaiah Scroll, which contains the entirety of the Book of Isaiah, dating around 125-100 B.C.E. Comparing these ancient copies with the later Masoretic Text reveals an extraordinary level of consistency, validating the preservation of the Hebrew Bible over centuries and affirming the faithfulness of its transmission. For instance, Isaiah 40:8 declares, "The grass withers, the flower fades, but the word of our God will stand forever," a statement exemplified by the enduring reliability of the text over time.

Sectarian Writings: Insights into the Qumran Community's Beliefs

The sectarian writings provide details about the unique beliefs, practices, and laws that governed the Qumran community. These texts, such as the *Community Rule, Damascus Document,* and the *War Scroll,* elucidate the strict codes of conduct and purity laws that the community adhered to, emphasizing a high standard of righteousness, which they believed distinguished them from a corrupt religious establishment. The writings also include teachings of the Teacher of Righteousness, a prophetic leader who interpreted the Scriptures for the community and served as a guide in their pursuit of covenantal loyalty to Jehovah.

The *Community Rule*, in particular, provides insight into the organizational structure, worship practices, and initiation rites of the Qumran sect. This document highlights the sect's commitment to maintaining ritual purity, obedience to a strict interpretation of the Mosaic Law, and separation from the wider Jewish community, which they perceived as apostate.

Other Literature: Commentary and Reflection

The Dead Sea Scrolls also contain non-sectarian works, including psalms, hymns, and apocalyptic literature, which reflect the community's eschatological beliefs and their view of divine intervention. The *Habakkuk Commentary*, for example, contains an interpretation of the Book of Habakkuk, viewed by the Qumran community as foretelling contemporary events relevant to their religious struggles. This interpretive method, in which ancient prophecies were applied to the community's own circumstances, reflects a view that divine judgment was imminent, targeting the "Wicked Priest" and those seen as compromising Jehovah's law.

What Was the Significance of the Scrolls' Location Near the Dead Sea?

The location of the Qumran community near the Dead Sea is significant for several reasons. The arid conditions of the Judean Desert, which preserved the scrolls over the centuries, allowed for their remarkable survival, while the remoteness of Qumran underscores the sect's commitment to separation from the broader society. By distancing themselves physically and spiritually, the community sought to create a purified environment for the worship of Jehovah.

The physical setting of Qumran near the Dead Sea may have been chosen for both symbolic and practical reasons. The Dead Sea, a place of extreme isolation and lifelessness, represents a boundary from the rest of society, reflecting the Qumran community's self-imposed separation and their belief in spiritual purity. This isolation aligned with their theological conviction that they alone were the true followers of Jehovah, distinct from the compromised religious practices of Jerusalem and its Temple, which they viewed as defiled. As Isaiah 52:11 exhorts, "Depart, depart, go out from there; touch no unclean thing; go out from the midst of her; purify yourselves, you who bear the vessels of Jehovah."

How Do the Scrolls Reflect the Qumran Community's View of Prophecy and Divine Revelation?

The Qumran community's writings reveal a unique approach to prophecy and divine revelation, seeing themselves as the heirs of the prophets of Israel. They believed that Jehovah had granted them special insight into the Scriptures through their Teacher of Righteousness, who, they claimed, was endowed with the ability to interpret hidden prophecies. This role of prophetic interpretation was fundamental to their understanding of current events, particularly in relation to the perceived corruption of the Jerusalem priesthood.

For the Qumran community, prophecy was not confined to past historical events but was applicable to their present circumstances and future expectations. They believed that certain prophecies contained coded messages or esoteric meanings that could only be understood by the righteous remnant. This interpretative approach, found in the *Habakkuk Commentary* and other texts, portrayed the Qumran community as the faithful elect awaiting Jehovah's judgment upon the apostate religious establishment.

The Teacher of Righteousness: A Divinely Inspired Interpreter of Prophecy

One of the most prominent figures in the sectarian writings is the Teacher of Righteousness, whom the community saw as a divinely inspired interpreter of prophecy. The Teacher's interpretations of the Hebrew Scriptures offered insight into the Qumran community's eschatological expectations and reinforced their belief in a coming divine judgment against those who had strayed from covenantal purity. This figure held a prophetic role within the community, guiding their interpretation of the Scriptures and solidifying their identity as a people set apart.

This approach to prophecy demonstrates the community's conviction that they were living in the "last days," a time in which the promises and warnings of the Scriptures were being fulfilled. The Teacher's interpretations connected their own experience with that of Israel's ancient prophets, such as Isaiah and Jeremiah, who had similarly warned against apostasy and urged a return to Jehovah's covenant.

How the Dead Sea Scrolls Contribute to Our Understanding of Jewish Thought in the Second Temple Period

The Dead Sea Scrolls provide critical insights into Jewish thought during the Second Temple period, a time characterized by a diversity of religious beliefs and sects. The Qumran community, as revealed in the scrolls, represents one of several groups that sought to preserve what they viewed as the purity of Jehovah's covenant in the face of widespread apostasy. This period was marked by tensions between various Jewish sects, each claiming exclusive fidelity to the Mosaic Law and competing for religious authority within Jewish society.

The sectarian writings indicate that the Qumran community viewed itself as the faithful remnant in contrast to groups like the Pharisees and Sadducees, who held positions of power within the temple and broader society. Their focus on ritual purity, strict observance of the Sabbath, and distinct dietary laws reflects a broader trend within Second Temple Judaism toward maintaining an identity set apart for Jehovah.

The scrolls also offer insight into early Jewish eschatological beliefs. The Qumran community's writings reflect a heightened awareness of divine judgment and an expectation of imminent intervention by Jehovah. Their apocalyptic worldview, as evidenced in the *War Scroll* and other texts, reveals an intense expectation of a final confrontation between the forces of righteousness and wickedness, with Jehovah delivering victory for His faithful remnant. This eschatological hope underscores the centrality of divine justice within their beliefs and their anticipation of the establishment of a purified, covenantally faithful Israel.

The Preservation of the Scrolls: Testament to Their Beliefs and Determination

The survival of the Dead Sea Scrolls is a testament to the Qumran community's commitment to preserving their beliefs. They stored these texts in clay jars and hid them in caves, seemingly anticipating a time when their words would need protection from persecution or destruction. This deliberate act of preservation reflects a deep conviction that their writings contained truths worth safeguarding for future generations. By concealing these texts in remote desert caves, the community displayed a commitment to ensuring that their interpretation of Jehovah's covenantal faithfulness would survive.

In considering this careful preservation, the words of Psalm 119:89 come to mind: "Forever, O Jehovah, your word is firmly fixed in the heavens." The community's actions echo this belief in the eternal significance of God's word, as they sought to ensure the endurance of their teachings even beyond their lifetimes. The Dead Sea Scrolls, thus, serve as both an archaeological artifact and a testimony to the Qumran community's dedication to what they viewed as the true worship of Jehovah.

The Scrolls' Contribution to Biblical Studies and the Reliability of Scripture

The Dead Sea Scrolls have profoundly impacted biblical studies by providing the earliest copies of many books of the Hebrew Bible, confirming the reliability of the Masoretic Text. These scrolls affirm that the Hebrew Scriptures were transmitted with remarkable accuracy, despite centuries of copying and recopying. This transmission fidelity supports the belief in the Scriptures as inspired and preserved by Jehovah for the instruction of His people.

The scrolls also illuminate the diversity of Jewish thought in the Second Temple period, offering a broader context for understanding the historical and religious background of early Jewish sects and their relationship with Jehovah's covenant. The Qumran community's focus on covenant loyalty and purity resonates with the Scriptural exhortation in Deuteronomy 6:5-6: "You shall love Jehovah your God with all your heart and with all your soul and with all your might. And these words that I command you today shall be on your heart."

Through the lens of the Dead Sea Scrolls, we gain a fuller understanding of the passion and devotion that characterized this community's pursuit of Jehovah's commandments, as well as the enduring relevance of their faith in a time of religious conflict and upheaval.[1]

---

[1] *THE DEAD SEA SCROLLS: What Is the Truth About the Dead Sea Scrolls?* – August 20, 2024, by Edward D. Andrews (Author)

CHAPTER 3 The Damascus Document: First Glimpses of the Teacher of Righteousness

The Damascus Document: An Essential Text for Understanding the Qumran Community

The *Damascus Document*, one of the most pivotal texts found among the Dead Sea Scrolls, offers an essential first look into the beliefs, practices, and leadership of the Qumran community. It introduces us to their strict adherence to the Mosaic Law and their deep commitment to the pursuit of righteousness and covenantal loyalty. The document provides foundational insights into the Teacher of Righteousness, an enigmatic figure revered by this community, whose life and teachings were instrumental in shaping the Qumran sect's worldview and religious practices. The document itself serves as a covenantal guide, delineating both the requirements and expectations that the community held as followers of Jehovah's commandments.

What Is the Damascus Document, and Why Is It Important?

The *Damascus Document*, also known as the *Covenant of Damascus*, is a text that articulates the Qumran community's understanding of covenantal faithfulness. Originally discovered in the Cairo Genizah in the late 19th century, additional copies were later found at Qumran, establishing its significance within the Dead Sea Scrolls collection. The text serves as both a theological and practical guide, detailing the community's beliefs and outlining specific regulations and instructions that members were to follow. The document also includes admonitions against what it considers apostate Jewish groups, underscoring the community's desire for purity and separation from what they viewed as corrupted practices.

This text's covenantal language connects deeply to the Hebrew Bible's emphasis on loyalty to Jehovah, echoing verses like Deuteronomy 7:9, which says, "Know therefore that Jehovah your God is God, the faithful God who keeps covenant and steadfast love with those who love him and keep his commandments, to a thousand generations." The Qumran community viewed themselves as the true remnant, striving to uphold this loyalty even as they observed the widespread apostasy around them.

How Does the Damascus Document Introduce the Teacher of Righteousness?

Within the *Damascus Document*, the Teacher of Righteousness is introduced as a prophetic leader chosen by Jehovah to guide the community back to a faithful observance of His covenant. The Teacher's identity remains unspecified, yet his significance is undeniable. According to the document, the Teacher was an inspired interpreter of Scripture, responsible for revealing hidden truths and guiding the community in their spiritual journey. This portrayal resonates with the figure of a divinely appointed prophet, reminiscent of Old Testament leaders who called the people back to faithfulness, such as Elijah, who confronted idolatry, and Ezra, who led a return to strict adherence to the Law.

The Teacher of Righteousness is depicted as a man who possessed an unparalleled understanding of the Law, viewing the Scriptures not as mere historical records but as dynamic texts with direct application to the lives of Jehovah's people. His role as an interpreter of divine truth positioned him as the central religious authority within the Qumran sect. The *Damascus Document* thus provides the first essential glimpse into his teachings and the community's conviction that he was chosen by Jehovah to restore righteousness amid a time of profound spiritual decline.

The Teacher's Call to Righteousness and Covenant Loyalty

The *Damascus Document* emphasizes that the Teacher of Righteousness led his followers in a path of strict obedience to Jehovah's commandments, aligning with the concept of righteousness as an essential characteristic of those who are faithful to the covenant. This call to righteousness is not merely a moral exhortation but a covenantal obligation, one that carries profound implications for the community's relationship with Jehovah. The document reflects the belief that righteousness is achieved through complete submission to God's Law and separation from the corrupted practices of the outside world.

The text's description of the Teacher of Righteousness underscores his role as one who led by example, embodying the purity and commitment he preached. In the document's view, righteousness was not an optional attribute but a fundamental requirement for those who desired fellowship with Jehovah. As Proverbs 2:20-21 states, "So you will walk in the way of the good and keep to the paths of the righteous. For the upright will inhabit the land, and those with integrity will remain in it." This verse encapsulates the Qumran community's belief that righteousness was the only path to divine favor, a belief that the Teacher of Righteousness continually emphasized.

The Teacher as Interpreter of Prophecy and Guide to Scriptural Truth

One of the defining features of the Teacher of Righteousness, as presented in the *Damascus Document*, is his ability to interpret prophecy. The community saw him as uniquely gifted in understanding the hidden meanings within Scripture, an insight they believed was divinely granted. This interpretive authority was central to his role within the community, as his teachings provided both clarity and direction to his followers regarding the prophetic texts that they believed applied directly to their circumstances.

The Qumran community's emphasis on prophecy is evident throughout the *Damascus Document*. The Teacher's interpretations often cast their own community as the faithful remnant and the broader Jewish establishment as having fallen into apostasy. In this context, the Teacher of Righteousness is viewed as a latter-day prophet, akin to Isaiah or Jeremiah, whose teachings reflect Jehovah's will and whose interpretations reveal the community's place in the unfolding plan of God. Isaiah 30:21 echoes this sense of divine guidance, "And your ears shall hear a word behind you, saying, 'This is the way, walk in it,' when you turn to the right or when you turn to the left."

Through his interpretive teachings, the Teacher gave the community a framework for understanding their role as the chosen remnant, set apart to uphold Jehovah's covenant. His teachings were not speculative but grounded in a detailed, careful examination of Scripture, resonating with the Qumran community's strict adherence to a literal interpretation of the Law.

Opposition to Apostasy: The Teacher's Denunciation of Corruption

The *Damascus Document* also provides evidence of the Teacher's confrontational stance against those he viewed as corrupt. He was not merely a passive figure but an active opponent of what he considered the pervasive apostasy within mainstream Jewish leadership, particularly those associated with the temple in Jerusalem. The Teacher of Righteousness denounced the temple authorities as corrupt, accusing them of straying from Jehovah's commandments and compromising the holiness of Israel's worship.

The document's language regarding apostasy is strong, reflecting the Qumran community's belief that true faithfulness to Jehovah required absolute separation from those who had defiled the covenant. This sentiment aligns with passages such as Jeremiah 7:9-10, where Jehovah reproaches the people for violating His commandments, saying, "Will you steal, murder, commit adultery, swear falsely, make offerings to Baal, and go after other gods that you have not known, and then come and stand before me in this house, which is called by my name, and say, 'We are delivered!' only to go on doing all these abominations?"

For the Teacher of Righteousness and his followers, it was intolerable to allow these abominations to persist within their community, leading them to withdraw and establish a distinct religious society grounded in purity and strict adherence to the Law.

Purity and Separation: The Community's Commitment Under the Teacher's Guidance

Central to the *Damascus Document* is the community's rigorous approach to purity and separation from the wider Jewish society, reflecting their conviction that they were the true remnant of Israel. This notion of separation is consistent with the teachings of the Teacher of Righteousness, who stressed the importance of holiness and adherence to Jehovah's Law as prerequisites for maintaining the covenant. Under his guidance, the community instituted a range of purity laws, from dietary restrictions to ritual washings, aimed at preserving their status as the elect of Jehovah.

These purity regulations were not arbitrary but were believed to be essential for anyone seeking a relationship with God. The Qumran community's strict interpretation of the Law required them to avoid all forms of contamination, both physical and spiritual, as illustrated in passages such as Leviticus 20:26, "You shall be holy to me, for I Jehovah am holy and have separated you from the peoples, that you should be mine." This call to holiness encapsulates the essence of the Teacher's instruction, as he urged his followers to distance themselves from all practices they deemed unholy.

The community's belief in purity extended beyond ritual observances to encompass every aspect of life, from interpersonal relationships to religious observance. They viewed themselves as the sole guardians of Jehovah's covenant, a role that they took with utmost seriousness under the leadership of the Teacher of Righteousness.

The Promise of Divine Vindication for the Faithful

The *Damascus Document* contains a strong eschatological element, reflecting the Teacher's conviction that Jehovah would ultimately vindicate His people by judging the apostate groups and restoring the true remnant to a place of honor. The Qumran community saw themselves as this faithful remnant, set apart by Jehovah and awaiting the fulfillment of His promises. This expectation of divine vindication was an integral part of their identity, reinforcing their commitment to the covenant despite the challenges they faced.

The Teacher's teachings included assurances that Jehovah would one day deliver His people and execute judgment upon the corrupt religious authorities, aligning with passages such as Isaiah 35:4, which declares, "Say to those who have an anxious heart, 'Be strong; fear not! Behold, your God will come with vengeance, with the recompense of God. He will come and save you.'" The Qumran community held tightly to this hope, believing that their faithfulness to the Law would ultimately result in divine favor and protection in the day of Jehovah's judgment.

The *Damascus Document* is thus both a guide for holy living and a prophetic text, offering hope and encouragement to the Qumran community as they awaited Jehovah's vindication. The Teacher of Righteousness instilled in his followers the confidence that their efforts to uphold the Law would not be in vain, providing them with a theological foundation for enduring persecution and maintaining their covenantal loyalty.

The Role of the Damascus Document in Establishing the Teacher's Authority

Through the *Damascus Document*, the Qumran community established the Teacher of Righteousness as their central religious figure, whose teachings provided both the moral and theological framework for their distinct way of life. His authority was not based on institutional power but on his unparalleled understanding of Scripture and his commitment to Jehovah's covenant. This document serves as a testament to his role in shaping the community's beliefs, as his interpretations and exhortations became the foundation for their religious identity.

The Teacher's role as both a guide and an interpreter is encapsulated in the document's presentation of his teachings, revealing his deep impact on the Qumran sect's perception of faithfulness. His life, dedicated to the pursuit of holiness and the denouncement of apostasy, became the model for his followers, who saw him as the true embodiment of covenant loyalty.

The *Damascus Document* provides a vivid portrayal of the Teacher of Righteousness as a man chosen by Jehovah to lead His people in a time of spiritual crisis, a leader whose life and teachings continue to offer profound insights into the values that defined the Qumran community's pursuit of divine truth.

CHAPTER 4 The Community Rule: Establishing Order and Righteousness

Introduction to the Community Rule: A Foundational Text for the Qumran Community

The *Community Rule*, one of the essential texts within the Dead Sea Scrolls, is a profound testament to the values, beliefs, and organizational principles that guided the Qumran sect. This document, known in Hebrew as *Serekh ha-Yahad*, serves as a constitution for the Qumran community, outlining its laws, codes of conduct, organizational structure, and spiritual principles. Through this document, we gain insight into the sect's rigorous commitment to living as a "holy community" devoted to Jehovah's covenant. The Community Rule is not merely a collection of rules but a covenantal framework, setting the foundation for the sect's collective identity, values, and purpose.

The *Community Rule* emphasizes the necessity of purity, obedience, and righteousness, establishing an order that is both organizational and spiritual. It underscores the community's view that they alone upheld the true covenant with Jehovah, a conviction that justified their separation from mainstream Jewish society. This belief is vividly expressed in passages that emphasize the community's role as a "house of holiness" and an "everlasting planting" (cf. Isaiah 61:3). This text is pivotal in understanding the community's distinct lifestyle, which centered on absolute loyalty to Jehovah and the unrelenting pursuit of righteousness.

The Covenant and Commitment to Holiness in the Community Rule

The central theme of the *Community Rule* is the covenantal relationship between Jehovah and the Qumran sect, who saw themselves as a faithful remnant set apart to maintain purity in a time of spiritual decline. This covenant, which the members pledged to uphold, was both individual and communal, binding each member to a life of righteousness, submission to divine law, and separation from sin.

The Qumran community viewed their covenant as a direct continuation of the covenant established at Mount Sinai, where Jehovah commanded His people to live according to His laws. The text echoes this sentiment, exhorting its members to commit wholeheartedly to the observance of the Law and to avoid any practice that might compromise their purity. This aligns with the command in Deuteronomy 6:5, "You shall love Jehovah your God with all your heart and with all your soul and with all your might," a verse that encapsulates the sect's approach to covenant loyalty.

The Role of the Teacher of Righteousness in the Community's Structure and Law

In the context of the *Community Rule*, the Teacher of Righteousness is portrayed as an essential figure who provided divine insight and interpretation of the Law. Though not explicitly named in every section of this document, his influence permeates the text, as it reflects his teachings on righteousness, purity, and order. His role extended beyond that of a mere leader; he was regarded as a divinely appointed interpreter, whose understanding of the Scriptures set the foundation for the community's code of conduct.

The Teacher's teachings, which emphasized the uncompromising observance of Jehovah's law, were foundational to the sect's identity. His authority in interpreting Scripture guided the community in applying the principles of the Law to their unique circumstances, effectively serving as a safeguard against deviation from Jehovah's commandments. His role resonates with the figure of a prophet or sage, reminiscent of leaders like Ezra, who "set his heart to study the Law of Jehovah, and to do it and to teach his statutes and rules in Israel" (Ezra 7:10).

Establishing Order Through Hierarchical Structure and Accountability

The *Community Rule* outlines a strict hierarchical structure within the Qumran sect, reinforcing the importance of order and discipline. The community's organizational structure was intended to reflect a microcosm of divine order, with clear roles and responsibilities assigned to each member. The highest authority within the community was held by the priests, followed by Levites, and then lay members, each with specific functions and levels of accountability. This hierarchy ensured that each member contributed to the collective holiness and order of the group, and it reflected the sect's belief in divine organization.

The text describes a system of "overseers" or "inspectors" who were responsible for maintaining discipline, instructing members in the Law, and guiding them in the path of righteousness. These overseers were expected to embody the community's values, serving as examples of moral integrity and spiritual maturity. They played a crucial role in upholding the community's high standards, ensuring that each member adhered to the rules and regulations of the covenant. This structure reinforced the community's focus on order, discipline, and mutual accountability, aligning with the biblical principle found in Proverbs 27:17, "Iron sharpens iron, and one man sharpens another."

The concept of accountability within the Qumran sect extended beyond mere organizational function; it was a spiritual discipline that promoted the community's pursuit of righteousness. Members were required to submit to regular assessments of their conduct and adherence to the Law, fostering an environment of transparency and spiritual growth. The system of accountability, as prescribed in the *Community Rule*, reflects the sect's understanding of the covenant as a collective responsibility, where each member's faithfulness contributed to the community's overall purity.

Ritual Purity and Separation from Outsiders

One of the most distinctive aspects of the *Community Rule* is its emphasis on ritual purity and the need for separation from outsiders, particularly those whom the sect regarded as defiled or apostate. This principle of separation was not rooted in personal animosity but in a theological conviction that the Qumran community represented the true Israel, called to uphold a higher standard of holiness. Members of the community were required to observe strict purity laws, abstaining from practices or associations that might contaminate their spiritual standing.

The document's prescriptions for purity were extensive, encompassing dietary laws, cleanliness rituals, and Sabbath observance. This emphasis on purity reflects the community's adherence to Leviticus 11:44, "For I am Jehovah your God. Consecrate yourselves therefore, and be holy, for I am holy." The Qumran sect's commitment to ritual purity served as both a symbolic and practical expression of their devotion to Jehovah, reinforcing their identity as a holy community set apart from the world.

This separation from outsiders extended to all areas of life, from worship practices to communal meals. The sect's meals were considered sacred, with specific regulations governing who could participate and how the food was to be prepared and consumed. Participation in these communal meals was restricted to those who had undergone purification rites, underscoring the community's understanding of fellowship as an act of worship. These practices echo the biblical call to holiness and separation, as seen in passages like Numbers 6:2-5, which outline the Nazirite vow as a commitment to personal holiness.

Discipline and Expulsion: Maintaining Purity and Order Within the Community

The *Community Rule* includes detailed provisions for the discipline and, if necessary, expulsion of members who failed to adhere to the community's standards. This approach to discipline reflects the Qumran sect's belief that the purity of the community must be preserved at all costs, even if it required the removal of members who posed a spiritual threat. Offenses were categorized by severity, with corresponding punishments ranging from temporary restrictions to permanent expulsion.

The process of discipline was designed to encourage repentance and restoration whenever possible. Members who transgressed were given opportunities to demonstrate genuine repentance, often through fasting, isolation, or other acts of penitence. This approach reflects the community's commitment to upholding righteousness while also allowing for the possibility of redemption. However, for those who refused to repent or repeatedly violated the covenant, expulsion was the final measure, as the community could not tolerate ongoing impurity within its ranks. This concept aligns with the biblical principle found in 1 Corinthians 5:6-7, which warns, "Do you not know that a little leaven leavens the whole lump? Cleanse out the old leaven that you may be a new lump, as you really are unleavened."

The sect's approach to discipline underscores the high value it placed on purity and the belief that even one person's sin could compromise the sanctity of the entire community. This principle of corporate responsibility is seen in the *Community Rule*'s emphasis on collective accountability, where each member's conduct had an impact on the community as a whole.

Commitment to Prayer, Study, and Communal Living

The Qumran community's commitment to prayer, Scriptural study, and communal living is evident throughout the *Community Rule*, which describes these practices as central to their religious life. The community's daily routine was structured around these spiritual disciplines, which they believed were essential to maintaining their covenantal relationship with Jehovah. Prayer was not merely a personal practice but a collective act of devotion, often conducted in unison as a means of reinforcing their unity and commitment to Jehovah.

Scriptural study held a prominent place within the community, as members were expected to engage in regular reflection on the Law and the Prophets. This study was guided by the interpretations provided by the Teacher of Righteousness, whose teachings served as a lens through which the community understood the Scriptures. The community's focus on Scriptural study aligns with passages such as Psalm 1:2, which describes the righteous as those who "delight in the law of Jehovah, and on his law he meditates day and night."

Communal living was another defining feature of the Qumran sect, as members shared their possessions and resources, creating an environment of mutual support and accountability. This practice of shared living was not motivated by material necessity but by a theological conviction that their lives should reflect the unity and purity of the covenant community. The *Community Rule* provides detailed guidelines on the communal distribution of resources, emphasizing the principle of equality and the belief that each member's well-being contributed to the community's overall holiness. This approach to communal living echoes the spirit of Acts 4:32, where the early Christian community is described as being "of one heart and soul," sharing all things in common.

The Eschatological Vision and Hope in the Community Rule

The *Community Rule* includes an eschatological vision that reveals the community's hope for the future and their belief in Jehovah's impending judgment on the wicked. The Qumran sect viewed themselves as living in the last days, anticipating a divine intervention that would vindicate their commitment to righteousness and bring about the establishment of Jehovah's kingdom. This expectation of judgment and deliverance shaped their worldview, reinforcing their commitment to purity and separation from what they viewed as a corrupt society.

This eschatological hope is expressed in the language of the *Community Rule*, which describes the community as a "preparation for the day of vengeance." The community believed that Jehovah's judgment was imminent and that they were called to prepare themselves for this event through lives of holiness and obedience. This anticipation of divine justice is consistent with passages such as Isaiah 66:15-16, which proclaim, "For behold, Jehovah will come in fire, and his chariots like the whirlwind, to render his anger in fury, and his rebuke with flames of fire. For by fire will Jehovah enter into judgment."

The *Community Rule*'s eschatological vision provided the Qumran community with a sense of purpose and destiny, as they saw themselves as participants in Jehovah's unfolding plan. This hope for divine intervention was not merely an abstract belief but a motivating force that shaped every aspect of their lives, from their dedication to the Law to their separation from apostate practices.

Conclusion: The Role of the Community Rule in Shaping the Qumran Sect

The *Community Rule* stands as a profound document that encapsulates the values, beliefs, and practices of the Qumran community. Through its detailed regulations, hierarchical structure, emphasis on purity, and eschatological hope, this text provides a comprehensive picture of the community's commitment to covenant loyalty and righteousness. The Community Rule reveals a group that viewed themselves as the true Israel, chosen by Jehovah to uphold His commandments in a time of widespread apostasy.

The Qumran community's adherence to the *Community Rule* reflects their unwavering devotion to Jehovah's covenant, as they sought to live lives marked by holiness, obedience, and hope. In examining this document, we gain insight into the spiritual and theological foundation of the Qumran sect, whose pursuit of righteousness remains a testament to their belief in Jehovah's promises.

CHAPTER 5 The Habakkuk Commentary: Conflict with the Wicked Priest

Introduction to the Habakkuk Commentary: A Text of Conflict and Prophetic Interpretation

The *Habakkuk Commentary*, one of the pivotal sectarian texts among the Dead Sea Scrolls, is an interpretative manuscript that expounds on the book of Habakkuk in the Hebrew Bible while drawing parallels to the experiences of the Qumran community. This commentary, also known as *Pesher Habakkuk*, serves as a historical lens through which the Teacher of Righteousness and the Wicked Priest are portrayed as conflicting figures, each representing opposing forces within the religious and social landscape of the time. The *Habakkuk Commentary* captures the depth of this rivalry, not only highlighting their theological differences but also the consequences of spiritual apostasy and corruption within Israel.

In this text, the Teacher of Righteousness is presented as a leader appointed by Jehovah to interpret prophetic scriptures, leading his followers in a path of covenantal faithfulness. By contrast, the Wicked Priest is depicted as a morally compromised figure associated with the corrupt religious establishment in Jerusalem. This document reveals a profound tension, as the Teacher and his followers are set against the forces of apostasy that the Wicked Priest embodies. Through its interpretation of Habakkuk, the *Pesher* provides insight into the eschatological outlook, ethical values, and divine expectations that defined the Qumran community's belief system.

What Is the Habakkuk Commentary, and How Does It Reflect the Sect's Beliefs?

The *Habakkuk Commentary* follows a unique interpretative style known as *pesher*, a method by which ancient prophecies were applied to contemporary situations. The Qumran community believed that they were living in a time of fulfillment, with many prophecies finding immediate relevance in their lives. This *pesher* method of interpretation allowed the community to apply Habakkuk's warnings and judgments to their own experiences, portraying the Teacher of Righteousness and the Wicked Priest as figures within this divine narrative.

In using the book of Habakkuk as a basis, the commentary provides a critique of those who have forsaken Jehovah's covenant, identifying them with the religious authorities in Jerusalem. This interpretative approach shows the community's conviction that they were the faithful remnant amid a spiritually corrupt society. Their understanding of Habakkuk's prophecies echoes the Qumran sect's expectation of divine retribution against those who have turned from the Law, fulfilling the prophet's words, "For still the vision awaits its appointed time… if it seems slow, wait for it; it will surely come; it will not delay" (Habakkuk 2:3). The Teacher's role in applying these prophecies to the community's context demonstrates his profound authority as an interpreter of divine revelation.

The Teacher of Righteousness: Interpreter of Prophecy and Leader of the Faithful Remnant

Within the *Habakkuk Commentary*, the Teacher of Righteousness is depicted as a figure of immense authority, charged with the responsibility of revealing Jehovah's will to his followers. His interpretative role reflects the community's belief that Jehovah had granted him special insight into the Scriptures, enabling him to uncover the hidden meanings within the prophetic texts. The Teacher's interpretations were seen as divinely inspired, guiding the Qumran community in understanding their position as Jehovah's chosen remnant.

The Teacher's interpretations went beyond the surface meaning of the text, often unveiling a message of imminent judgment upon those who had corrupted Jehovah's covenant. In this sense, he stands in the tradition of the Old Testament prophets, who called Israel back to righteousness and warned of the consequences of apostasy. His role as an interpreter is evident in the commentary's application of Habakkuk's words, where the teacher draws parallels between the prophet's warnings and the corruption he perceived within the temple establishment. As Proverbs 3:5-6 reminds, "Trust in Jehovah with all your heart, and do not lean on your own understanding. In all your ways acknowledge him, and he will make straight your paths." The Teacher's role as an interpreter embodies this trust in divine wisdom, offering his followers a clear understanding of Jehovah's expectations.

Through his interpretation of Habakkuk, the Teacher of Righteousness fortified his community's identity as a people set apart, providing them with a sense of purpose and mission. His teachings emphasized a life of purity, obedience, and loyalty to Jehovah's commandments, reflecting the community's understanding of themselves as a faithful remnant awaiting divine vindication.

The Wicked Priest: Symbol of Apostasy and Corruption

In stark contrast to the Teacher of Righteousness, the Wicked Priest is portrayed in the *Habakkuk Commentary* as a corrupt leader who embodies spiritual decay and moral compromise. The Wicked Priest's identity is not specified within the text, but he is frequently associated with the religious authorities in Jerusalem who, in the view of the Qumran community, had forsaken the true covenant. The Wicked Priest's actions are described in terms that highlight his disregard for the sanctity of the Law and his willingness to engage in practices that the community considered abominable.

The *Habakkuk Commentary* accuses the Wicked Priest of "walking in the ways of falsehood" and "defiling the sanctuary of Jehovah." This depiction aligns with the community's view of the Jerusalem priesthood as being tainted by political ambition, greed, and a disregard for purity. The figure of the Wicked Priest thus serves as a symbol of everything the Qumran sect rejected—apostasy, corruption, and compromise with secular power. This criticism resonates with the biblical warning in Isaiah 1:23, "Your princes are rebels and companions of thieves. Everyone loves a bribe and runs after gifts. They do not bring justice to the fatherless, and the widow's cause does not come to them."

The community's portrayal of the Wicked Priest underscores their sense of separation from the established religious authorities, whom they viewed as having abandoned Jehovah's commandments. This adversarial stance reinforced the Qumran sect's identity as a purified community, distinct from the compromised leadership in Jerusalem.

The Conflict Between the Teacher of Righteousness and the Wicked Priest: A Struggle for Covenant Faithfulness

The *Habakkuk Commentary* describes an intense conflict between the Teacher of Righteousness and the Wicked Priest, presenting their struggle as a cosmic battle between righteousness and apostasy. This conflict was not merely a theological disagreement but a profound clash of values, with each figure representing opposing interpretations of Jehovah's covenant. The Teacher of Righteousness, as a faithful interpreter of the Law, saw himself as upholding the true essence of the covenant, while the Wicked Priest, in his pursuit of power and disregard for purity, was portrayed as a betrayer of that covenant.

According to the *Habakkuk Commentary*, the Wicked Priest actively opposed the Teacher of Righteousness, attempting to undermine his authority and harm him. The text recounts how the Wicked Priest "pursued" the Teacher of Righteousness, seeking to suppress his teachings and influence. This pursuit is symbolic of the broader opposition faced by the Qumran community, as they viewed themselves as a persecuted remnant standing firm against apostate forces. This struggle is reminiscent of the trials faced by Old Testament prophets like Elijah, who confronted the idolatrous practices of Israel's leadership (1 Kings 18:17-18).

The Teacher's response to this persecution was not one of retaliation but of continued faithfulness to the covenant. By remaining steadfast in his interpretation of the Law, he exemplified the community's commitment to righteousness, even in the face of hostility. This conflict ultimately underscored the community's belief that righteousness must be pursued at all costs, as seen in passages like Psalm 37:39-40, "The salvation of the righteous is from Jehovah; he is their stronghold in the time of trouble. Jehovah helps them and delivers them."

The Eschatological Significance of the Teacher-Wicked Priest Conflict

The *Habakkuk Commentary* frames the conflict between the Teacher of Righteousness and the Wicked Priest within an eschatological context, reflecting the Qumran community's belief in an impending divine judgment. The community held that Jehovah would soon intervene to vindicate the righteous and punish the wicked, bringing about the fulfillment of His promises. This expectation of divine retribution was central to their identity, reinforcing their commitment to the covenant as they awaited Jehovah's intervention.

The commentary interprets Habakkuk's warnings of judgment as directly applicable to their own time, identifying the Wicked Priest and his followers as targets of divine wrath. The text describes a future day when Jehovah will "destroy the assembly of the wicked," a prophecy that the community believed was directed toward the corrupt priesthood. This eschatological perspective served as a source of hope for the Qumran sect, affirming their belief that their faithfulness would ultimately be rewarded. Passages like Isaiah 35:4, "Say to those who have an anxious heart, 'Be strong; fear not! Behold, your God will come with vengeance, with the recompense of God. He will come and save you,'" encapsulate the community's anticipation of divine justice.

The eschatological theme within the *Habakkuk Commentary* illustrates the community's conviction that the struggle between the Teacher and the Wicked Priest was part of a larger cosmic battle between righteousness and evil. This perspective provided the

Qumran sect with a sense of purpose, as they saw themselves as active participants in Jehovah's redemptive plan.

Divine Judgment and the Fate of the Wicked Priest

The *Habakkuk Commentary* portrays the Wicked Priest's eventual downfall as an act of divine judgment, underscoring the Qumran community's belief in Jehovah's justice. The text describes the Wicked Priest as one who would ultimately face the consequences of his actions, with Jehovah intervening to deliver retribution upon him. This depiction aligns with the community's understanding of divine justice, where those who violate the covenant are held accountable before God.

The judgment against the Wicked Priest serves as a warning to all who compromise their loyalty to Jehovah for personal gain. The Qumran community believed that their commitment to righteousness would be vindicated through Jehovah's intervention, while the apostate leaders would face destruction. This view resonates with the assurance found in Proverbs 21:12, "The Righteous One observes the house of the wicked; he throws the wicked down to ruin."

For the Qumran sect, the fate of the Wicked Priest was a reminder of Jehovah's sovereignty and His commitment to upholding the covenant. This divine judgment reinforced their understanding of righteousness as a covenantal requirement, emphasizing that faithfulness would ultimately be rewarded, while apostasy would lead to ruin.

Conclusion: The Habakkuk Commentary as a Reflection of the Community's Struggle for Righteousness

The *Habakkuk Commentary* serves as a powerful reflection of the Qumran community's commitment to righteousness and their belief in Jehovah's justice. Through its portrayal of the conflict between the Teacher of Righteousness and the Wicked Priest, this text offers profound insight into the sect's theological convictions and their understanding of covenant faithfulness. The *Habakkuk Commentary* reveals a community that viewed themselves as the faithful remnant, standing in opposition to a corrupt religious establishment as they awaited divine vindication.

This document not only captures the Qumran sect's eschatological hope but also their sense of moral purpose, as they sought to live according to Jehovah's commandments despite the challenges they faced. Through the lens of the *Habakkuk Commentary*, we gain a deeper understanding of the Teacher of Righteousness and his role in guiding the community toward a life of covenant loyalty, purity, and unwavering faith in Jehovah's promises.

CHAPTER 6 The Identity Debate: Who Was the Teacher of Righteousness?

Introduction to the Identity Debate of the Teacher of Righteousness

The identity of the Teacher of Righteousness, one of the central figures in the Dead Sea Scrolls, has been the subject of much debate and speculation among scholars. This leader, revered by the Qumran community, is portrayed as a prophetic figure chosen by Jehovah to guide a faithful remnant amid widespread apostasy within the Jewish religious establishment. The Teacher of Righteousness is depicted as a man of deep spiritual insight, divinely appointed to reveal hidden truths in the Scriptures and lead his followers in a life of covenantal fidelity.

Through various texts, including the *Damascus Document* and *Habakkuk Commentary*, the Teacher of Righteousness is presented as one who understood Jehovah's will and interpreted the Law in ways that distanced the Qumran community from what they viewed as a corrupt priesthood in Jerusalem. However, despite the significance of this figure, his precise identity remains elusive. Some scholars have speculated that he was an influential Jewish priest, while others have questioned whether he might have been a precursor to Jesus. Nevertheless, careful analysis of theological, historical, and scriptural evidence indicates clear distinctions between the Teacher of Righteousness and the person of Jesus.

What Do the Dead Sea Scrolls Reveal About the Teacher of Righteousness?

The Dead Sea Scrolls portray the Teacher of Righteousness as a man who possessed profound knowledge of the Law and prophetic writings. He is consistently depicted as a religious leader who urged strict adherence to Jehovah's commandments and was instrumental in interpreting prophetic texts that the Qumran community believed applied to their time. The Teacher is frequently referenced in texts that emphasize righteousness, purity, and devotion, and he is credited with establishing a covenantal community centered on these values.

The *Damascus Document* portrays the Teacher of Righteousness as a priestly figure who led his followers in resisting the "Wicked Priest" and those whom the community saw as violators of the true covenant. His teachings and interpretations provided the Qumran sect with a framework for understanding their role as a holy remnant amid the perceived spiritual decline of mainstream Judaism. In this context, the Teacher's life and teachings were foundational for the Qumran community, shaping their religious practices and expectations.

Passages within the *Damascus Document* also suggest that the Teacher faced persecution from the religious authorities in Jerusalem, whom the Qumran sect believed had compromised their covenant with Jehovah. This portrayal resonates with Old Testament themes where prophets often confronted Israel's leaders, calling them to repentance and warning them of divine judgment. Thus, the Teacher of Righteousness embodies the prophetic tradition of urging faithfulness to Jehovah, emphasizing a life of holiness, obedience, and unwavering commitment to the Law. His message is reminiscent of passages like Isaiah 1:16-17, which exhorts, "Wash yourselves; make yourselves clean; remove the evil of your deeds from before my eyes; cease to do evil, learn to do good; seek justice, correct oppression."

Theories Regarding the Teacher's Identity

Several theories have emerged regarding the historical identity of the Teacher of Righteousness, each grounded in interpretations of the historical context of the Second Temple period. While none of these theories can be proven with certainty, they provide insight into the complexity of this figure and the theological significance he held for the Qumran community.

Theory 1: A High Priest Displaced by Political Corruption

One theory suggests that the Teacher of Righteousness may have been a high priest who was deposed from his position by rivals within the priesthood. According to this view, the Teacher of Righteousness was originally a legitimate high priest who sought to uphold the purity of temple worship and the Law but was replaced by individuals who were more politically aligned with Hellenistic influences and secular authorities. The Dead Sea Scrolls frequently accuse the Jerusalem priesthood of corruption, associating them with the Wicked Priest, whom the community saw as a violator of Jehovah's covenant.

The *Habakkuk Commentary* reflects the Qumran community's belief that the Wicked Priest pursued the Teacher of Righteousness, persecuting him for his adherence to the Law and his refusal to compromise with secular authorities. If the Teacher was indeed a high priest, this would align with the community's perception that their leader was a victim of injustice, a man who had been displaced for upholding righteousness. This portrayal echoes passages such as Psalm 94:20-21, which ask, "Can wicked rulers be allied with you, those who frame injustice by statute? They band together against the life of the righteous and condemn the innocent to death."

Theory 2: A Zadokite Priest from a Purist Sect

Another theory identifies the Teacher of Righteousness as a Zadokite priest, possibly descended from the priestly line of Zadok, whom Jehovah had appointed to serve in the temple during the time of King David and Solomon (cf. 1 Kings 2:35). The Zadokites were traditionally regarded as legitimate temple priests, and some scholars suggest that the Qumran community saw themselves as heirs to this priestly line, maintaining the purity and sanctity of temple worship in contrast to the Hellenistic influences they viewed as corrupting the priesthood in Jerusalem.

This theory is supported by the Qumran community's focus on priestly purity and ritual observance, which they believed the mainstream priesthood had abandoned. The *Community Rule* and *Damascus Document* reveal the community's rigorous commitment to purity, a commitment that the Teacher of Righteousness is believed to have embodied. This connection to the Zadokite line would explain why the Qumran sect distanced themselves from the Jerusalem temple and established their own worship practices, aligning with their belief that they represented the true Israel. Ezekiel 44:15 captures this ideal of a faithful priesthood: "But the Levitical priests, the sons of Zadok, who kept the charge of my sanctuary when the people of Israel went astray from me, shall come near to me to minister to me."

Theory 3: A Messianic Forerunner but Not the Messiah

The Qumran community held a high view of the Teacher of Righteousness, believing him to be divinely appointed and uniquely inspired, yet there is no indication in the Dead Sea Scrolls that they regarded him as the Messiah. Rather, the Teacher appears to have been seen as a forerunner—a prophetic figure preparing the way for the fulfillment of Jehovah's promises. Some passages suggest that the community expected a future Messiah who would deliver Israel and restore true worship, but the Teacher of Righteousness himself did not fulfill this role.

This distinction is crucial, as it clarifies that the Qumran community did not view the Teacher of Righteousness in the same way that Christians view Jesus. While both the Teacher and Jesus emphasized righteousness and adherence to divine law, Jesus explicitly identified Himself as the Messiah, the Son of God, and the means by which salvation would be accomplished. The Teacher of Righteousness, by contrast, did not claim this identity, nor did he fulfill the redemptive role attributed to Jesus. Isaiah 40:3 foreshadows this preparatory role: "A voice cries: 'In the wilderness prepare the way of Jehovah; make straight in the desert a highway for our God.'"

Why the Teacher of Righteousness and Jesus Are Not the Same Figure

Though some scholars have drawn parallels between the Teacher of Righteousness and Jesus, there are significant theological and historical differences that distinguish these two figures. The Teacher of Righteousness, as presented in the Dead Sea Scrolls, was a priestly and prophetic leader within the Qumran sect, emphasizing strict adherence to the Mosaic Law and separation from perceived apostasy. Jesus, however, brought a message that went beyond legalistic observance, offering Himself as the fulfillment of the Law and the pathway to reconciliation with God.

The Teacher's Need for Personal Purification Versus Jesus' Sinlessness

The Teacher of Righteousness, like all members of the Qumran community, adhered to rigorous purity laws, recognizing his own need for atonement and sanctification. The Qumran community emphasized frequent ritual cleansing as a means of maintaining spiritual purity, reflecting their belief in the fallibility of even their leaders. By contrast, Jesus was sinless and without the need for purification, as Paul affirms in 2 Corinthians 5:21: "For our sake he made him to be sin who knew no sin, so that in him we might become the righteousness of God." This essential distinction underscores that while the Teacher led his followers in righteousness, he did not possess the sinless nature that defined Jesus.

The Absence of Messianic Claims by the Teacher of Righteousness

The Dead Sea Scrolls do not depict the Teacher of Righteousness as claiming to be the Messiah, nor do they present him as one who would redeem others through a sacrificial death. Jesus, by contrast, explicitly identified Himself as the Messiah and ultimately offered Himself as a sacrificial atonement for sin, fulfilling the role of the Lamb of God (John 1:29). The Teacher of Righteousness did not claim to fulfill such a role; his leadership focused on guiding a remnant community in covenant faithfulness rather than providing a universal means of redemption.

The Resurrection: A Defining Difference

The defining difference between Jesus and the Teacher of Righteousness lies in the resurrection. According to Christian faith, Jesus rose from the dead, offering definitive proof of His divinity and His role as the Savior of all humankind. This event established Him as the "firstfruits of those who have fallen asleep" (1 Corinthians 15:20). There is no indication that the Teacher of Righteousness was resurrected, nor was resurrection a significant feature of the Qumran community's hope in the same way it became for early Christianity. The resurrection of Jesus affirmed His divine nature and mission, separating Him fundamentally from the Teacher of Righteousness, whose role was confined to that of a temporal leader and interpreter within a specific Jewish sect.

Conclusion: Understanding the Teacher of Righteousness as a Historical Figure

The Teacher of Righteousness remains an influential and revered figure within the Dead Sea Scrolls, embodying the Qumran community's dedication to covenant faithfulness, purity, and prophetic insight. While his identity cannot be definitively proven, the various theories regarding his background highlight the complexities of his role and the theological significance he held for his followers. The Teacher's life and teachings continue to offer valuable insights into the religious environment of the Second Temple period, shedding light on the values and beliefs that defined the Qumran community.

In examining the differences between the Teacher of Righteousness and Jesus, we gain a clearer understanding of the distinct roles they played within their respective communities. Though both figures emphasized righteousness, their missions, claims, and theological implications diverge significantly. The Teacher of Righteousness remains a testament to the Qumran community's pursuit of purity and obedience, while Jesus stands as the fulfillment of Jehovah's promises, providing a pathway to salvation for all who believe in Him.

CHAPTER 7 Righteousness and Covenant: Central Teachings of the Teacher

Introduction: The Centrality of Righteousness and Covenant to the Qumran Community

Among the Qumran community, the teachings of the Teacher of Righteousness regarding righteousness and covenantal loyalty were not mere moral guidelines but formed the core of their relationship with Jehovah. The Teacher emphasized that righteousness was both the foundation of the covenant and the primary expression of faithfulness. Unlike the religious establishment, which the Qumran sect believed had strayed into spiritual compromise, the Teacher of Righteousness urged his followers to uphold a strict interpretation of the Law, making righteousness a hallmark of their covenantal identity.

In the Hebrew Scriptures, righteousness is consistently tied to one's standing before Jehovah and obedience to His Law, a theme that is evident throughout the Teacher's teachings. Passages like Deuteronomy 6:25 illustrate this by affirming, "And it will be righteousness for us, if we are careful to do all this commandment before Jehovah our God, as he has commanded us." For the Teacher of Righteousness, such adherence to the Law was not only an individual endeavor but a collective calling, binding the Qumran community in a shared pursuit of holiness and purity.

The Teacher's View of Righteousness: Beyond Ritual to Spiritual Integrity

In the teachings of the Teacher of Righteousness, righteousness was far more than ritual adherence to the Law; it was a deep, transformative commitment that impacted every aspect of life. The

Teacher saw righteousness as a comprehensive lifestyle of obedience, purity, and separation from the sins and compromises prevalent within mainstream Judaism. The *Community Rule* and other Qumran texts reflect his belief that true righteousness was found in an unwavering commitment to Jehovah's commandments, untainted by the world's influence.

This understanding of righteousness as an all-encompassing lifestyle aligns with the exhortation in Psalm 15:2-3, which states, "He who walks blamelessly and does what is right and speaks truth in his heart; who does not slander with his tongue and does no evil to his neighbor." The Teacher's emphasis on internal purity as well as external obedience illustrates his belief that righteousness required both a right heart and right actions. For the Qumran community, this meant cultivating a personal and communal identity that stood in stark contrast to the religious establishment, which they believed had compromised with secular powers.

The Covenant as a Binding Agreement of Holiness and Separation

The Teacher of Righteousness viewed the covenant with Jehovah as a sacred, unbreakable agreement that demanded total loyalty and obedience from its members. This covenant was not merely a set of rules but a divine relationship that called the community to holiness and separation from sin. The Qumran community saw themselves as the true Israel, bound by a covenant that was established not only in ritual but in the entirety of their way of life.

The *Community Rule* reflects this perspective, describing the Qumran sect as "children of light" who were to keep themselves unstained by the "sons of darkness." This terminology echoes the contrast found in passages like Deuteronomy 7:6, which states, "For you are a people holy to Jehovah your God. Jehovah your God has chosen you to be a people for his treasured possession, out of all the peoples who are on the face of the earth." The Teacher's interpretation of the covenant emphasized that this chosenness came with an obligation to live in righteousness and obedience, setting them apart as a remnant faithful to Jehovah.

Righteousness as a Path of Humility, Submission, and Obedience

The Teacher of Righteousness emphasized that true righteousness required humility, submission, and obedience to Jehovah's will. This was not a righteousness derived from one's own accomplishments but one granted by Jehovah through faithful adherence to His commandments. The Qumran community saw themselves as humble servants, whose role was to maintain the integrity of the covenant even when others strayed.

In the *Damascus Document*, the Teacher's teachings encourage his followers to "walk in humility" and to "serve in the truth," underscoring the importance of humility as an aspect of righteousness. This perspective is consistent with passages such as Micah 6:8, which declares, "He has told you, O man, what is good; and what does Jehovah require of you but to do justice, and to love kindness, and to walk humbly with your God?" For the Teacher, humility was not weakness but a recognition of one's dependence on Jehovah and a commitment to submitting to His authority.

This humility was also reflected in the community's view of themselves as a faithful remnant, set apart not by their own merit but by their willingness to obey Jehovah in a time of apostasy. The Teacher's emphasis on humility served as a constant reminder that righteousness was not merely about outward observance but about a heart devoted to following Jehovah's ways.

The Community's Commitment to Righteousness Through Purity Laws

The Qumran community's commitment to righteousness was expressed through strict purity laws, which the Teacher of Righteousness believed were essential for maintaining covenantal loyalty. The Teacher taught that purity was not only a matter of personal holiness but a means of preserving the sanctity of the community. The *Community Rule* includes detailed prescriptions for ritual cleanliness, dietary restrictions, and Sabbath observance, all of which were seen as expressions of their devotion to Jehovah.

The emphasis on purity reflects the Qumran community's understanding of passages like Leviticus 20:26, which commands, "You shall be holy to me, for I Jehovah am holy and have separated you from the peoples, that you should be mine." For the Qumran sect, purity was both a personal responsibility and a communal safeguard, protecting the entire community from the defilement of sin. The Teacher's teachings on purity served as a reminder that righteousness required constant vigilance against any influence that could corrupt their covenant with Jehovah.

The Covenant as a Source of Eschatological Hope

The Teacher of Righteousness taught that the covenant with Jehovah was not only a present obligation but a source of future hope. He believed that Jehovah would ultimately vindicate His faithful remnant, rewarding their commitment to righteousness and delivering them from the corrupt influences of the world. This eschatological hope was central to the Qumran community's identity, giving them the strength to endure persecution and maintain their commitment to the covenant.

In the *Habakkuk Commentary*, the Teacher interprets the prophecies of Habakkuk as foretelling a time of divine intervention when Jehovah would judge the wicked and restore righteousness to His people. This expectation resonates with passages such as Isaiah 35:4, which says, "Say to those who have an anxious heart, 'Be strong; fear not! Behold, your God will come with vengeance, with the recompense of God. He will come and save you.'" For the Qumran community, the covenant was a promise that their faithfulness would not go unrewarded, and the Teacher's teachings reinforced their confidence in Jehovah's future deliverance.

This eschatological perspective gave the Qumran community a sense of purpose, as they saw themselves as participants in a divine plan that would ultimately culminate in the restoration of righteousness. The Teacher's emphasis on covenantal loyalty as a path to future hope distinguished the Qumran sect from the religious establishment, which they believed had lost sight of the true meaning of the covenant.

The Role of the Teacher of Righteousness as a Guide to the True Covenant

The Teacher of Righteousness saw his role as one of guiding his followers back to the true meaning of the covenant, which he believed had been distorted by the mainstream religious authorities. He emphasized that the covenant required more than ritual observance; it demanded a heart committed to Jehovah and a life that reflected His holiness. Through his interpretations and teachings, the Teacher provided his followers with a framework for understanding and living out the covenant, preserving its purity in a time of spiritual decline.

The Teacher's role as a guide reflects the call in passages like Jeremiah 3:15, which says, "And I will give you shepherds after my own heart, who will feed you with knowledge and understanding." For the Qumran community, the Teacher of Righteousness was a divinely appointed shepherd who led them in the path of covenant faithfulness, offering them a way of life that stood in contrast to the compromises they observed in the religious establishment.

By upholding the covenant's requirements for purity, righteousness, and separation from sin, the Teacher reinforced the community's identity as a faithful remnant, set apart to fulfill Jehovah's purpose. His teachings provided them with a clear understanding of what it meant to live as people of the covenant, rooted in obedience and loyalty to Jehovah's commandments.

Righteousness and Covenant as Interdependent Aspects of Faithfulness

The Teacher of Righteousness taught that righteousness and covenant were interdependent, each reinforcing and giving meaning to the other. For the Qumran community, righteousness was the outward expression of their covenant with Jehovah, while the covenant provided the framework for understanding and pursuing righteousness. This interdependence emphasized that righteousness was not an isolated virtue but a direct response to the covenantal relationship with Jehovah.

This perspective is reflected in passages like Deuteronomy 10:12-13, which says, "And now, Israel, what does Jehovah your God require of you, but to fear Jehovah your God, to walk in all his ways, to love him, to serve Jehovah your God with all your heart and with all your soul, and to keep the commandments and statutes of Jehovah, which I am commanding you today for your good?" For the Teacher of Righteousness, righteousness was inseparable from covenantal loyalty, each reinforcing the other as essential components of faithfulness.

The Qumran community's understanding of righteousness and covenant as interdependent aspects of faithfulness distinguished them from the mainstream religious authorities, whom they believed had forsaken the true meaning of the covenant. This emphasis on righteousness as a covenantal requirement underscored their commitment to a life of purity, obedience, and separation from sin.

Conclusion: The Enduring Legacy of the Teacher's Teachings on Righteousness and Covenant

The Teacher of Righteousness remains a profound figure in the Dead Sea Scrolls, offering a model of covenant faithfulness that defined the Qumran community's way of life. Through his teachings on righteousness and covenant, he provided his followers with a clear understanding of what it meant to live as a holy remnant, separated from the compromises of the world. His emphasis on purity, humility, obedience, and eschatological hope reflects a commitment to Jehovah that continues to resonate as a powerful example of faithfulness.

For the Qumran community, the Teacher's teachings on righteousness and covenant were not abstract ideals but concrete principles that shaped their daily lives, offering them a path of devotion that they believed would lead to Jehovah's ultimate vindication. His role as an interpreter of Scripture, a guide to holiness, and a guardian of the covenant underscores the significance of his message, revealing the depth of his influence on those who sought to follow Jehovah with unwavering devotion.

Edward D. Andrews

CHAPTER 8 The Eschatological Vision of the Teacher of Righteousness

Introduction: The Teacher of Righteousness and His Eschatological Worldview

The Teacher of Righteousness is often considered one of the most pivotal figures within the Qumran community, not only because of his teachings on covenant and righteousness but also due to his eschatological vision. The Teacher presented a worldview wherein he and his followers were participants in a cosmic struggle between the forces of good and evil. The Qumran sect's understanding of the end times, shaped by the Teacher's interpretations, positioned them as the righteous remnant destined to witness Jehovah's decisive judgment upon a corrupt world. This eschatological framework was foundational to the community's identity, instilling in them a sense of purpose, urgency, and spiritual vigilance.

The eschatological outlook fostered by the Teacher was one of anticipation and preparation. He interpreted the prophetic Scriptures with an eye toward imminent fulfillment, identifying specific enemies of the covenant and outlining the traits that would characterize the final battle between righteousness and apostasy. This vision of the future influenced every aspect of the community's life, from their rituals and strict adherence to the Law to their separation from the mainstream religious authorities in Jerusalem. The Teacher's eschatological teachings formed the backbone of the Qumran community's identity, shaping their understanding of both present trials and future hopes.

The Role of Prophetic Scriptures in the Teacher's Eschatology

The Teacher of Righteousness held a distinctive role as the community's primary interpreter of the Hebrew Scriptures, especially the prophetic texts that contained promises of Jehovah's coming judgment. His eschatology was deeply rooted in a historical-grammatical interpretation of texts like Isaiah, Jeremiah, and Habakkuk, which he applied directly to the circumstances of his own time. The Teacher believed that these prophecies foretold a period of divine intervention, where Jehovah would destroy the wicked and establish a purified community of the faithful.

The *Habakkuk Commentary*, for example, reveals the Teacher's interpretative approach, in which he reads the prophet's warnings of judgment as applying specifically to the religious authorities and nations opposing the Qumran community. The Teacher identified his enemies, such as the Wicked Priest, within these prophetic frameworks, viewing them as embodiments of the opposition that the faithful would encounter before Jehovah's intervention. In Isaiah 13:11, the prophet declares, "I will punish the world for its evil, and the wicked for their iniquity; I will put an end to the pomp of the arrogant, and lay low the pompous pride of the ruthless." The Teacher's eschatological teachings reflected his conviction that this divine judgment was imminent and that his community would witness the fulfillment of these prophecies.

Through this eschatological lens, the Teacher urged his followers to live as though the end was near, a call that required strict adherence to the covenant and a readiness to endure trials. His interpretations reinforced the Qumran sect's understanding of themselves as the chosen remnant, set apart to inherit Jehovah's promises.

The Teacher's View of Divine Judgment and the Fate of the Wicked

Central to the Teacher of Righteousness's eschatological teachings was the belief in an impending divine judgment against those who had forsaken the covenant. The Teacher asserted that Jehovah's judgment was not arbitrary but was a righteous response to the sins and unfaithfulness of those who had defiled the Law. He described this judgment in vivid terms, warning that the wicked, including the compromised priesthood in Jerusalem, would face the consequences of their actions.

The Teacher's portrayal of divine judgment was both retributive and purifying. He envisioned a day when Jehovah would not only destroy the wicked but also refine His people, preserving a faithful remnant that would inherit His promises. This perspective aligns with passages like Malachi 3:2-3, which declares, "For he is like a refiner's fire and like fullers' soap. He will sit as a refiner and purifier of silver, and he will purify the sons of Levi and refine them like gold and silver." For the Teacher of Righteousness, this purification was essential to restoring the covenant and establishing a community free from corruption.

In his eschatological vision, the Teacher emphasized that Jehovah's judgment would be swift and thorough, leaving no room for repentance among those who had abandoned His Law. He warned his followers to separate themselves from these individuals, lest they also face divine retribution. This expectation of judgment reinforced the Qumran community's commitment to a life of holiness, as they sought to ensure their own purity in anticipation of Jehovah's coming wrath upon the unfaithful.

The Eschatological Conflict: A Battle Between Light and Darkness

The Teacher's eschatology presented the end times as a cosmic battle between forces of light and darkness, a theme that permeated Qumran literature. In this view, the community of the faithful, led by the Teacher of Righteousness, represented the forces of light, while the enemies of the covenant, including the Wicked Priest, were seen as the embodiment of darkness. This dualistic framework underscored the Teacher's belief in an absolute distinction between the righteous and the wicked, with no room for compromise or middle ground.

The *War Scroll*, another key text within the Dead Sea Scrolls, details this final battle, portraying the Qumran community as participants in an eschatological war where Jehovah would ultimately triumph over His enemies. Though not authored by the Teacher of Righteousness himself, the *War Scroll* echoes his eschatological vision, depicting a struggle between the "sons of light" and the "sons of darkness." This dualism aligns with passages like Isaiah 60:2, which contrasts the darkness covering the earth with the light that arises upon Jehovah's people: "For behold, darkness shall cover the earth, and thick darkness the peoples; but Jehovah will arise upon you, and his glory will be seen upon you."

The Teacher's emphasis on this cosmic struggle reinforced the Qumran sect's sense of purpose, as they saw themselves as soldiers in a divine conflict that would culminate in the defeat of evil and the establishment of Jehovah's kingdom. This battle between light and darkness was not merely a future event but a present reality, as the community sought to live as agents of Jehovah's light amid a world overshadowed by sin.

The Role of the Teacher as a Watchman and Prophetic Guide

In the Teacher of Righteousness's eschatological vision, he saw himself as a watchman—a role that involved vigilance, discernment, and warning his followers of impending dangers. His teachings reflect a prophetic responsibility to prepare the community for the trials they would face in the last days, urging them to remain faithful to Jehovah and vigilant against the temptations of apostasy.

The Teacher's role as a watchman aligns with the prophetic tradition seen in Ezekiel 33:7, where Jehovah says, "So you, son of man, I have made a watchman for the house of Israel. Whenever you hear a word from my mouth, you shall give them warning from me." The Teacher's interpretations of the Scriptures and his warnings about the Wicked Priest and other enemies of the covenant were consistent with this responsibility. His guidance provided the Qumran community with both a clear understanding of the threats they faced and a vision of the righteousness required to withstand them.

The Teacher's watchfulness also extended to his expectation of specific signs that would herald the arrival of Jehovah's judgment. His teachings encouraged his followers to recognize these signs and to be prepared for the trials that would accompany the end times. This vigilance was a means of reinforcing the community's commitment to the covenant, as they sought to live in a state of readiness, anticipating the fulfillment of Jehovah's promises.

The Promise of Vindication for the Faithful Remnant

In his eschatological teachings, the Teacher of Righteousness emphasized that Jehovah would ultimately vindicate His faithful remnant, delivering them from persecution and rewarding their commitment to the covenant. This promise of vindication was a source of hope for the Qumran community, as they believed that their faithfulness would not go unnoticed. The Teacher assured his followers that Jehovah's judgment would not only punish the wicked but also establish His people in righteousness, fulfilling His promises to the faithful.

The Teacher's confidence in Jehovah's vindication of the righteous resonates with passages like Isaiah 62:11-12, which declares, "Behold, Jehovah has proclaimed to the end of the earth: Say to the daughter of Zion, 'Behold, your salvation comes; behold, his reward is with him, and his recompense before him.' And they shall be called The Holy People, The Redeemed of Jehovah." For the Qumran community, the Teacher's eschatology was not only a call to vigilance but also an assurance that their faithfulness would be rewarded.

This promise of vindication reinforced the community's identity as a chosen remnant, set apart to witness Jehovah's judgment upon the unfaithful and to inherit His blessings. The Teacher's teachings on vindication provided the Qumran sect with a sense of purpose, as they endured persecution and maintained their commitment to the covenant in anticipation of Jehovah's deliverance.

The Eschatological Hope of Restoration and Renewal

The Teacher's eschatology did not focus solely on judgment; it also contained a vision of restoration and renewal. He taught that Jehovah's judgment would ultimately purify His people, creating a community that was free from corruption and wholly devoted to the covenant. This vision of a restored Israel was central to the Qumran community's hope, as they believed that their faithfulness would contribute to the establishment of a new order in which Jehovah's righteousness would reign.

The Teacher's hope for restoration echoes the promise in Isaiah 65:17-18, where Jehovah declares, "For behold, I create new heavens and a new earth, and the former things shall not be remembered or come into mind. But be glad and rejoice forever in that which I create." For the Qumran community, this renewal was not merely a distant hope but a goal that motivated their daily practices and commitment to the covenant. The Teacher's teachings instilled in them a vision of a future where righteousness would prevail, and they would be part of a purified community living in harmony with Jehovah's Law.

Conclusion: The Eschatological Vision as the Foundation of the Teacher's Message

The Teacher of Righteousness's eschatological vision was integral to his teachings, shaping the Qumran community's identity, practices, and hope for the future. By emphasizing divine judgment, the cosmic battle between light and darkness, and the promise of vindication and renewal, the Teacher provided his followers with a comprehensive understanding of their role in Jehovah's plan. His eschatology was both a call to vigilance and a source of hope, reinforcing the community's commitment to the covenant and their anticipation of Jehovah's ultimate victory.

Edward D. Andrews

CHAPTER 9 The Teacher's Interpretation of the Law

Introduction: The Teacher's Approach to the Law in the Qumran Community

The Teacher of Righteousness, a central figure within the Qumran community, viewed the Law as more than a mere set of ritual obligations; he saw it as the foundation of a covenantal relationship with Jehovah. His interpretation was guided by a conviction that strict adherence to the Law was necessary for righteousness and for maintaining a pure community, untainted by the spiritual compromises of the wider Jewish world. In his view, the Law was a divinely ordained path to sanctity, one that set apart the faithful remnant and preserved their distinct identity as Jehovah's people.

Within the Dead Sea Scrolls, particularly in texts like the *Damascus Document* and *Community Rule*, the Teacher's interpretations reflect an approach to the Law that balanced literal observance with a profound understanding of its spiritual implications. His teachings emphasized that the Law was not only a guide for individual behavior but a binding framework for the community's collective life. Through his interpretations, the Teacher reinforced a unique and rigorous view of the Law, one that demanded complete obedience and served as a bulwark against the religious corruption he believed had overtaken the mainstream Jewish leaders.

The Law as a Covenant of Holiness and Separation

For the Teacher of Righteousness, the Law was an expression of Jehovah's holiness and a covenant that required total separation from sin. The Qumran community viewed themselves as "sons of light," set apart from the world through obedience to the Law. In the Teacher's teachings, the Law represented a sacred agreement, a covenant that distinguished the faithful from the unfaithful and served as the foundation of a life in alignment with Jehovah's will.

The Teacher drew upon passages from the Hebrew Scriptures to reinforce this view, often invoking the covenantal language found in books like Deuteronomy and Leviticus. Leviticus 20:26, for example, commands, "You shall be holy to me, for I Jehovah am holy and have separated you from the peoples, that you should be mine." This idea of separation was central to the Teacher's interpretation, as he taught that the Qumran community was obligated to observe the Law with strict adherence to demonstrate their loyalty to Jehovah and maintain their distinctiveness as His people.

The Teacher's focus on separation was not limited to physical or ceremonial purity; it extended to a separation of values and practices. He interpreted the Law as a means of establishing a community identity distinct from the mainstream Jewish authorities, whom he saw as compromised and corrupt. This emphasis on holiness as separation shaped every aspect of the Qumran community's life, from dietary regulations to the Sabbath observance, all of which were grounded in a profound commitment to the Law as the guiding force for their lives.

The Teacher's Literal and Rigorous Interpretation of the Law

The Teacher of Righteousness is best understood as a literalist in his approach to the Law. His interpretation did not allow for compromise or relaxation of its requirements; rather, he believed that every commandment was to be followed with the utmost precision. This rigorous approach is evident in the community's strict observance of the Sabbath, dietary laws, and ritual purity. The Teacher taught that even minor deviations from the Law were acts of unfaithfulness, capable of endangering the entire community's relationship with Jehovah.

The Teacher's emphasis on strict observance resonates with passages such as Deuteronomy 5:32, which exhorts, "You shall be careful to do as Jehovah your God has commanded you. You shall not turn aside to the right hand or to the left." For the Qumran community, the Teacher's interpretations reinforced this command, instilling a conviction that strict adherence to the Law was essential for righteousness. This understanding fostered an environment where meticulous observance became a way of life, shaping the identity of the Qumran sect as a people wholly dedicated to Jehovah.

In texts like the *Community Rule*, the Teacher's strict interpretations are evident in the regulations governing purity, communal living, and worship practices. For instance, the community's approach to ritual purity involved regular cleansing rituals, dietary restrictions, and an avoidance of contact with outsiders, all of which reflected the Teacher's belief that the Law's requirements must be upheld without compromise. This level of adherence underscored the Teacher's conviction that the Law was not merely a set of guidelines but a divine mandate that governed every aspect of life within the Qumran community.

Interpretative Authority: The Teacher's Role as an Interpreter of the Law

The Teacher of Righteousness held a unique position within the Qumran community as both a prophet and an interpreter of the Law. He claimed divine authority to explain and apply the Law, often reinterpreting existing practices to align with what he viewed as Jehovah's true intentions. This interpretative authority was a cornerstone of his leadership, as he guided his followers in understanding the deeper meanings of the commandments and their application in the context of a covenantal community.

The Teacher's role as an interpreter is comparable to the authority seen in passages like Malachi 2:7, which states, "For the lips of a priest should guard knowledge, and people should seek instruction from his mouth, for he is the messenger of Jehovah of hosts." The Teacher saw himself as this kind of messenger, a custodian of divine knowledge who was uniquely positioned to interpret Jehovah's commandments. His interpretations were not presented as mere opinions but as authoritative clarifications, grounded in his deep understanding of the Scriptures and his conviction that he was divinely appointed to lead the Qumran community.

Through his interpretative authority, the Teacher not only reinforced the importance of adherence to the Law but also provided his followers with guidance on how to live out their covenantal responsibilities. His interpretations included specific regulations for community life, personal conduct, and religious observances, all aimed at fostering a community that was wholly aligned with Jehovah's will. This authoritative interpretation solidified the Teacher's role as a spiritual leader, one whose teachings on the Law shaped the Qumran sect's identity and purpose.

Purity Laws as a Means of Distinction and Covenant Fidelity

Among the Teacher's teachings, the emphasis on purity laws held particular significance. The Qumran community was known for its strict adherence to purity regulations, which they saw as essential for maintaining their covenantal relationship with Jehovah. These laws were not only about ritual cleanliness but were understood as expressions of faithfulness, acts that demonstrated their loyalty to Jehovah and their commitment to a life set apart from the world.

The Teacher's interpretation of purity laws was based on passages such as Numbers 19:20, which warns, "If the man who is unclean does not cleanse himself, that person shall be cut off from the midst of the assembly, since he has defiled the sanctuary of Jehovah." For the Qumran community, this command reinforced the necessity of remaining ritually clean, lest they jeopardize their standing within the covenant. The Teacher's emphasis on purity was not just a ceremonial obligation but a means of preserving the community's sanctity and ensuring that they remained a faithful remnant in the eyes of Jehovah.

This focus on purity laws also underscored the Teacher's belief in the Law's power to shape and protect the identity of the covenantal community. By adhering to these regulations, the Qumran sect maintained a clear separation from those who had compromised the Law, particularly the religious authorities in Jerusalem. The Teacher's teachings on purity served as a constant reminder of their distinctiveness as a people chosen to uphold Jehovah's standards, even in the face of opposition and persecution.

The Teacher's Emphasis on the Sabbath and the Call to Holy Rest

The Sabbath held a place of high importance within the Teacher's interpretation of the Law. Observing the Sabbath was seen not only as a commandment but as a reflection of Jehovah's creation and a sign of the covenant between Jehovah and His people. The Teacher taught that strict Sabbath observance was essential for maintaining covenantal faithfulness, emphasizing that the Sabbath was a day set apart for holy rest and worship.

The Teacher's views on the Sabbath align with the commandment in Exodus 31:13, where Jehovah declares, "Above all you shall keep my Sabbaths, for this is a sign between me and you throughout your generations, that you may know that I, Jehovah, sanctify you." For the Qumran community, Sabbath observance was a testament to their commitment to the Law and a visible expression of their dedication to Jehovah. The Teacher's interpretations provided specific guidelines for Sabbath observance, prohibiting certain activities and requiring communal worship, all of which reinforced the sanctity of the day.

This emphasis on the Sabbath was part of the Teacher's broader understanding of the Law as a covenantal requirement, one that demanded not only obedience but reverence. By observing the Sabbath with strict adherence, the Qumran community upheld their identity as a people consecrated to Jehovah, demonstrating their willingness to live in accordance with His commandments. The Teacher's teachings on the Sabbath reflected his view that obedience to the Law was not merely a duty but a means of drawing closer to Jehovah and participating in the holiness that the Sabbath embodied.

The Teacher's Condemnation of the Religious Establishment's Compromises

One of the defining aspects of the Teacher of Righteousness's interpretation of the Law was his opposition to the religious authorities in Jerusalem, whom he viewed as corrupt and compromised. The Teacher believed that the mainstream Jewish leaders had forsaken the true interpretation of the Law, adopting practices and interpretations that diluted its demands and led the people into apostasy. His criticism of the religious establishment reflected his commitment to a pure and uncompromising observance of the Law.

In passages like Ezekiel 22:26, which rebukes the leaders of Israel by saying, "Her priests have done violence to my law and have profaned my holy things. They have made no distinction between the holy and the common," the Teacher found support for his condemnation of the religious establishment. He saw the leaders' actions as a betrayal of the covenant, believing that they had allowed external influences to corrupt the Law's purity. This stance strengthened the Qumran community's resolve to separate themselves from mainstream Judaism, reinforcing their identity as a remnant committed to the Law.

The Teacher's criticism was not only directed at specific practices but at the underlying attitudes that he believed had led the religious establishment to compromise the Law. He warned his followers to remain vigilant against these influences, teaching that true faithfulness required a complete rejection of any practices that deviated from Jehovah's commandments. His interpretations provided the Qumran community with a framework for understanding their separation from the religious authorities as an act of obedience to the Law and a means of preserving their covenantal faithfulness.

The Law as a Source of Eschatological Hope

In addition to guiding the community's present conduct, the Teacher of Righteousness taught that the Law held eschatological significance. He believed that Jehovah's ultimate judgment would be based on adherence to the Law, and that the Qumran community's faithfulness would be rewarded in the end times. This eschatological hope gave the Qumran sect a sense of purpose and motivation, as they viewed their obedience to the Law as preparation for the coming judgment.

The Teacher's eschatological interpretation of the Law echoes passages like Isaiah 51:7, which says, "Listen to me, you who know righteousness, the people in whose heart is my law; fear not the reproach of man, nor be dismayed at their revilings." For the Qumran community, the Law was not only a present guide but a future promise, a guarantee that their faithfulness would lead to vindication. This hope reinforced their commitment to the Law, as they believed that Jehovah would ultimately judge them according to their obedience and reward them as His faithful remnant.

The Teacher's emphasis on the Law as a source of eschatological hope distinguished the Qumran community from other Jewish groups, as they saw themselves as participants in a divine plan that would culminate in the establishment of a purified Israel. This vision of the Law's ultimate fulfillment provided the community with a sense of destiny, as they sought to live in accordance with Jehovah's commandments in anticipation of the promised future.

CHAPTER 10 Prophetic and Priestly Authority: The Teacher's Spiritual Leadership

Introduction: The Teacher's Spiritual Authority in a Time of Division

The Teacher of Righteousness was a pivotal figure in the Qumran community, serving not only as an interpreter of the Law but also as a leader with both prophetic and priestly authority. His unique role set him apart, as he claimed a divine calling to lead the Qumran sect during a time of profound division and spiritual apostasy within Judaism. In his leadership, the Teacher asserted his authority based on a dual role, combining the functions of prophet and priest to guide his followers along the path of righteousness.

The Teacher's spiritual leadership emerged in response to the perceived corruption of the religious establishment, particularly the priesthood in Jerusalem. His critiques of the priestly authorities reveal his conviction that true spiritual leadership required purity, obedience to the Law, and a commitment to Jehovah's covenant. Through his teachings, the Teacher sought to redefine spiritual authority, contrasting the corrupted priesthood with his own role as a divinely appointed guide to righteousness.

The Prophetic Role of the Teacher: A Voice of Divine Revelation

One of the most striking aspects of the Teacher of Righteousness's authority was his claim to prophetic insight. The Qumran community believed that the Teacher was divinely inspired to interpret the Scriptures, providing them with a unique understanding of Jehovah's will. His role as a prophet involved not only the exposition of Scriptural truth but also the declaration of Jehovah's judgment against those who had strayed from the covenant.

In the *Habakkuk Commentary*, the Teacher of Righteousness is presented as one who reveals "the mysteries of the prophets," a phrase that underscores his role in bringing clarity to previously veiled truths. The Qumran community saw him as a mediator through whom Jehovah communicated His will, much like the prophets of the Hebrew Scriptures. This parallels with passages like Amos 3:7, which states, "For Jehovah does nothing without revealing his secret to his servants the prophets." The Teacher's prophetic authority was seen as a continuation of this tradition, where divine knowledge was entrusted to a chosen leader who would guide the faithful.

This prophetic role empowered the Teacher to interpret the events of his time through a Scriptural lens, identifying specific enemies of the covenant, such as the Wicked Priest. His declarations of judgment and calls for repentance reflect the same urgency found in the prophetic tradition, as he warned of the consequences of unfaithfulness and urged his followers to remain true to the covenant. The Teacher's authority as a prophet gave the Qumran community a sense of divine purpose, as they believed they were living in a period of revelation, where Jehovah's plan for the faithful remnant was being unveiled.

The Teacher's Claim to Priestly Authority: A Guardian of the Covenant

In addition to his prophetic role, the Teacher of Righteousness also claimed a priestly authority that was deeply tied to his mission of preserving the covenant. Unlike the mainstream Jewish priesthood, which the Qumran sect regarded as compromised and corrupt, the Teacher presented himself as a true priest of Jehovah, committed to maintaining the purity of worship and obedience to the Law. His priestly authority was not rooted in hereditary lineage but in his dedication to covenantal faithfulness and his role as a spiritual leader for the Qumran community.

The Teacher's priestly function was central to his leadership, as he took on responsibilities such as overseeing communal purity, enforcing the observance of the Law, and guiding the community in their rituals and worship practices. In the *Community Rule*, his role is described in terms that evoke the responsibilities of a priest, underscoring his commitment to creating a holy community that would be acceptable to Jehovah. This priestly role aligns with passages such as Malachi 2:7, which declares, "For the lips of a priest should guard knowledge, and people should seek instruction from his mouth, for he is the messenger of Jehovah of hosts." The Teacher saw himself as fulfilling this duty, providing instruction and ensuring that his followers adhered to the covenant's demands.

By claiming priestly authority, the Teacher distinguished himself from the corrupted priesthood of Jerusalem. He warned his followers that the mainstream priesthood had defiled the temple and abandoned their covenantal responsibilities. The Teacher's priestly role was therefore not merely ceremonial but a means of preserving the purity of the Qumran community, ensuring that they remained faithful to the Law despite the widespread apostasy around them.

The Teacher as an Expositor of Scriptural Mysteries

The Teacher of Righteousness's prophetic authority extended to his interpretation of the Scriptures, where he revealed what he considered the hidden meanings within the prophetic texts. His teachings provided the Qumran community with a unique understanding of the Scriptures, especially concerning eschatology and the coming judgment upon the wicked. The Teacher's expositions were seen as divinely inspired, allowing his followers to grasp the mysteries of Jehovah's plan in a way that the mainstream religious leaders could not.

The Teacher's approach to Scripture is evident in texts like the *Damascus Document*, where he expounds upon the requirements of the Law and the signs of the times. His interpretations often included specific prophecies regarding the enemies of the covenant, emphasizing that Jehovah's judgment was imminent. This role as an expositor aligns with the function of a prophet as described in passages like Jeremiah 23:28, where Jehovah commands, "Let the prophet who has a dream tell the dream, but let him who has my word speak my word faithfully." The Teacher's interpretations provided his followers with both a warning of impending judgment and a guide for faithful living.

By unveiling these Scriptural mysteries, the Teacher reinforced the Qumran community's sense of purpose, as they saw themselves as participants in Jehovah's unfolding plan. His teachings offered them a framework for understanding the events of their time, grounding their experiences within the prophetic tradition. This role as an expositor also elevated the Teacher's authority, as his followers looked to him for guidance in interpreting the Scriptures and understanding Jehovah's will.

The Teacher's Spiritual Leadership and the Call to Purity

Central to the Teacher's leadership was his emphasis on purity, both personal and communal. His priestly authority included the responsibility of ensuring that the Qumran community adhered to strict standards of holiness, a task that involved not only the observance of ritual purity but also the cultivation of moral integrity. The Teacher taught that purity was essential for maintaining the covenant, as it demonstrated a commitment to Jehovah's Law and distinguished the Qumran sect from the unfaithful.

In Leviticus 19:2, Jehovah commands, "You shall be holy, for I Jehovah your God am holy." The Teacher's focus on purity was a direct response to this command, as he believed that holiness was not optional but a requirement for those who wished to remain in covenant with Jehovah. His teachings on purity encompassed various aspects of life, from dietary restrictions to Sabbath observance, all of which were seen as expressions of faithfulness. Through his leadership, the Teacher reinforced the Qumran community's identity as a holy remnant, committed to upholding the standards of the covenant even in the face of opposition.

The Teacher's emphasis on purity also extended to his critique of the religious establishment, which he believed had defiled the temple and compromised their obligations to Jehovah. His calls for purity were a direct rebuke to the mainstream priesthood, as he warned his followers to avoid the corrupt practices that had infiltrated the religious authorities. Through his teachings, the Teacher provided the Qumran community with a vision of purity that went beyond ritual observance, encompassing a lifestyle of holiness that honored Jehovah.

The Teacher's Role as a Shepherd of the Faithful Remnant

As both a prophet and a priest, the Teacher of Righteousness took on the role of a shepherd, guiding his followers through the spiritual and moral challenges of their time. His leadership was not only about enforcing the Law but also about providing encouragement and reassurance to a community that saw itself as isolated and persecuted. The Teacher's teachings often included promises of Jehovah's vindication, as he reminded his followers that their faithfulness would be rewarded in the end.

The Teacher's role as a shepherd is reflected in passages like Ezekiel 34:11-12, where Jehovah declares, "For thus says Jehovah God: Behold, I, I myself will search for my sheep and will seek them out. As a shepherd seeks out his flock when he is among his sheep that have been scattered, so will I seek out my sheep." The Qumran community saw the Teacher as a fulfillment of this promise, a leader who cared for the faithful remnant and guided them in their pursuit of righteousness. His teachings provided them with a sense of security, as they believed that their obedience to the covenant would ultimately lead to Jehovah's protection and deliverance.

The Teacher's role as a shepherd also included warning his followers about the dangers they faced, particularly the threat posed by the Wicked Priest and other enemies of the covenant. His guidance helped the Qumran community navigate the challenges of living as a holy remnant, as he taught them to remain steadfast in their commitment to Jehovah despite the hostility of the outside world.

The Teacher's Authority as a Mediator of Jehovah's Will

In his dual role as prophet and priest, the Teacher of Righteousness served as a mediator between Jehovah and the Qumran community, conveying Jehovah's expectations and guiding his followers in their covenantal obligations. This mediating role was essential to the Teacher's authority, as he claimed to possess divine insight into Jehovah's will, which he shared with the community through his teachings and interpretations of the Law.

This mediating role is reflected in the priestly function described in passages like Numbers 16:47, where the priest "stood between the dead and the living, and the plague was stopped." The Teacher's role as a mediator was not only about imparting knowledge but about interceding on behalf of his followers, ensuring that they remained in covenant with Jehovah. His authority as a mediator was seen as divinely appointed, and the Qumran community viewed his teachings as an expression of Jehovah's will for His faithful remnant.

Through his role as a mediator, the Teacher reinforced the importance of obedience and loyalty to the covenant, teaching his followers that their relationship with Jehovah depended on their willingness to adhere to the Law. His guidance provided them with a clear understanding of their responsibilities, as he emphasized that covenantal faithfulness was not optional but a requirement for those who wished to receive Jehovah's favor.

The Impact of the Teacher's Spiritual Leadership on the Qumran Community

The Teacher of Righteousness's prophetic and priestly authority shaped the identity and purpose of the Qumran community, as his teachings provided them with a vision of life that was wholly devoted to Jehovah. Through his leadership, the Qumran sect developed a unique understanding of spiritual authority, one that was rooted in covenantal faithfulness, purity, and obedience to the Law. The Teacher's dual role as a prophet and priest allowed him to guide his followers with both divine insight and practical instruction, creating a community that was set apart from the compromised religious authorities.

In sum, the Teacher's spiritual leadership was characterized by a commitment to righteousness, a dedication to the Law, and a vision of purity that defined the Qumran community's identity. His teachings reinforced their belief that they were Jehovah's chosen remnant, called to uphold the covenant and to prepare for the day when Jehovah would vindicate the faithful and judge the unfaithful. Through his prophetic declarations and priestly guidance, the Teacher of Righteousness provided the Qumran community with a path of devotion that honored Jehovah and maintained the integrity of the covenant.

CHAPTER 11 The Wicked Priest and the Teacher of Righteousness: Theological Conflict

Introduction: The Genesis of Theological Conflict at Qumran

The theological conflict between the Teacher of Righteousness and the Wicked Priest lies at the heart of the Qumran community's history and identity. This clash was not merely a matter of personal rivalry but was deeply rooted in opposing understandings of the Law, purity, and covenantal faithfulness. The Qumran community revered the Teacher as a divinely appointed guide who upheld the purity of the Law. In contrast, they vilified the Wicked Priest as a figure who embodied apostasy, corruption, and betrayal of Jehovah's commandments. The theological disagreements that emerged between these two figures shaped the community's worldview, reinforcing its sense of separation from mainstream Judaism and strengthening its commitment to a covenantal way of life.

The theological conflict with the Wicked Priest became a defining moment in the Qumran community's history, clarifying for them the nature of true spiritual authority and the dangers of compromise. This chapter explores the nature of this conflict, examining how the Teacher's commitment to righteousness and purity was diametrically opposed to the Wicked Priest's practices and beliefs. Through an examination of their differences, we can gain a deeper understanding of the theological principles that guided the Qumran community and the role that this conflict played in solidifying their identity as a faithful remnant.

Who Was the Wicked Priest? Understanding His Role and Influence

The Wicked Priest is a figure mentioned multiple times in the Dead Sea Scrolls, particularly in the *Habakkuk Commentary*, where he is depicted as an antagonist to the Teacher of Righteousness. The title "Wicked Priest" itself is indicative of the Qumran community's view of this individual. They saw him as a leader who had abandoned Jehovah's commandments, embracing practices and beliefs that were contrary to the spirit of the Law. While the identity of the Wicked Priest has been the subject of much scholarly debate, it is commonly thought that he held a position of authority within the priestly hierarchy in Jerusalem.

The Qumran community believed that the Wicked Priest's corruption extended to both his personal conduct and his interpretation of the Law. This individual is depicted as one who desecrated the temple, possibly through accepting foreign influences or engaging in impure practices that compromised the sanctity of worship. In the eyes of the Qumran sect, the Wicked Priest embodied all that had gone wrong with the religious establishment in Jerusalem. His actions were seen as a direct affront to Jehovah's covenant, symbolizing a departure from true worship and an embrace of secular or politically motivated practices.

In texts such as the *Habakkuk Commentary*, the Wicked Priest is described as having persecuted the Teacher of Righteousness, attempting to undermine his authority and subdue his influence. This hostility further underscores the theological conflict between them, as it illustrates the lengths to which the Wicked Priest was willing to go to maintain his power. The Qumran community saw this as evidence of his unworthiness, a sign that his authority was based not on divine appointment but on corruption and worldly ambition.

The Teacher of Righteousness's Theological Stance: Upholding the Covenant and Purity

In stark contrast to the Wicked Priest, the Teacher of Righteousness was revered by the Qumran community as a figure who upheld the Law in its entirety, demonstrating an unwavering commitment to covenantal purity and obedience. His teachings emphasized the importance of separating oneself from sin and dedicating oneself fully to Jehovah. For the Teacher, the Law was not merely a set of rituals but a divine mandate that defined the very identity of Jehovah's chosen people. His interpretations and teachings were aimed at creating a community that would embody the principles of righteousness and holiness, thus maintaining their standing within Jehovah's covenant.

The Teacher's theological stance is best understood as one rooted in the belief that obedience to the Law was essential for maintaining a relationship with Jehovah. His teachings often invoked passages from the Hebrew Scriptures that emphasized the importance of holiness, such as Leviticus 19:2, which commands, "You shall be holy, for I Jehovah your God am holy." The Teacher's emphasis on holiness and purity extended to all aspects of life within the Qumran community, from ritual practices to ethical behavior. His teachings reinforced the idea that covenantal faithfulness required not only obedience to the Law but a heart fully dedicated to Jehovah.

This approach placed the Teacher in direct opposition to the Wicked Priest, whose actions the Qumran community viewed as a violation of the covenant. The Teacher's stance was one of absolute loyalty to Jehovah's commandments, rejecting any form of compromise or deviation. This strict adherence to the Law became a hallmark of the Qumran community's identity, as they believed that they were the true remnant, a people set apart to uphold the principles of righteousness that had been abandoned by the mainstream religious authorities.

Key Theological Disputes Between the Teacher of Righteousness and the Wicked Priest

The theological conflict between the Teacher of Righteousness and the Wicked Priest was characterized by several key disputes, each of which reflected their differing views on the nature of the Law, purity, and covenantal responsibility. These disputes highlight the fundamental differences between the Qumran community and the religious establishment in Jerusalem, as they reveal contrasting interpretations of what it meant to be faithful to Jehovah.

One of the primary areas of disagreement involved the concept of purity, both personal and communal. The Teacher of Righteousness emphasized the importance of ritual and moral purity, believing that any deviation from the Law would compromise the community's relationship with Jehovah. This perspective is echoed in passages like Numbers 19:20, which warns, "If the man who is unclean does not cleanse himself, that person shall be cut off from the midst of the assembly, since he has defiled the sanctuary of Jehovah." The Qumran community took such warnings seriously, adhering to strict purity laws as an expression of their commitment to holiness.

The Wicked Priest, on the other hand, was accused of disregarding these standards, engaging in practices that the Qumran community viewed as impure and unacceptable. His alleged desecration of the temple was seen as a direct affront to Jehovah, as it violated the sanctity of the very place where Jehovah's presence was believed to dwell. This violation was interpreted as a rejection of the covenant, a sign that the Wicked Priest had abandoned the principles of purity and holiness that defined the true worship of Jehovah.

Another point of theological conflict concerned the interpretation of the Law itself. The Teacher of Righteousness advocated a literal and rigorous adherence to the Law, believing that every commandment held a divine purpose and that obedience was essential for covenantal faithfulness. The Wicked Priest, however, was seen as one who distorted the Law, interpreting it in ways that suited his own interests and undermined its original intent. This deviation from the Law was perceived as an attempt to dilute its demands, leading the people away from true obedience and into a form of worship that was compromised by worldly influences.

The Role of Prophetic Authority in the Conflict

The Teacher of Righteousness's prophetic authority played a significant role in his conflict with the Wicked Priest. The Qumran community believed that the Teacher possessed a divinely appointed authority to interpret the Scriptures and reveal Jehovah's will. This prophetic role not only reinforced his position as a leader but also provided his followers with a sense of divine validation, as they believed that Jehovah was working through the Teacher to guide them in righteousness.

In texts like Amos 3:7, we see the principle that "Jehovah does nothing without revealing his secret to his servants the prophets." The Qumran community saw the Teacher as such a prophet, one who had been entrusted with the mysteries of the Law and the power to interpret Jehovah's commandments. This prophetic authority contrasted sharply with the Wicked Priest, whose authority was seen as rooted in corruption rather than divine appointment. The Teacher's role as a prophet not only set him apart from the Wicked Priest but also legitimized his critiques of the religious establishment, as his followers viewed his teachings as revelations from Jehovah.

The Teacher's prophetic authority also gave him the platform to denounce the Wicked Priest publicly, warning his followers about the dangers of apostasy and urging them to remain steadfast in their commitment to the covenant. This denunciation was not merely a personal attack but was framed as a prophetic declaration of Jehovah's judgment against the corruption of the priesthood. Through his role as a prophet, the Teacher provided his followers with a clear understanding of the theological conflict they were engaged in, reinforcing their belief that they were the faithful remnant, chosen to uphold Jehovah's standards in a world that had turned away from true righteousness.

The Consequences of Apostasy: The Teacher's Warnings Against the Wicked Priest

The Teacher of Righteousness frequently warned his followers about the consequences of apostasy, using the Wicked Priest as a cautionary example. The Qumran community believed that the Wicked Priest's actions would ultimately lead to Jehovah's judgment, as he had defiled the covenant and abandoned his responsibilities as a priest. The Teacher's warnings were intended to remind his followers of the seriousness of covenantal faithfulness, emphasizing that those who compromised the Law would face divine retribution.

Passages like Jeremiah 5:23-25 echo the Teacher's perspective, as Jehovah warns, "But this people has a stubborn and rebellious heart; they have turned aside and gone away. They do not say in their hearts, 'Let us fear Jehovah our God, who gives the rain in its season, the autumn rain and the spring rain, and keeps for us the weeks appointed for the harvest.' Your iniquities have turned these away, and your sins have kept good from you." The Teacher used similar language to emphasize that unfaithfulness would lead to a loss of Jehovah's blessings and ultimately to His judgment.

For the Qumran community, these warnings reinforced their commitment to the Teacher's teachings, as they believed that their separation from the mainstream religious authorities was a necessary step to avoid the fate of the Wicked Priest. The theological conflict between the Teacher and the Wicked Priest thus served as a constant reminder of the dangers of compromise, motivating the community to remain vigilant in their pursuit of righteousness and their rejection of any practices that could lead to apostasy.

The Teacher's Vision of Covenant Faithfulness as a Counter to the Wicked Priest's Influence

At the core of the theological conflict between the Teacher of Righteousness and the Wicked Priest was the concept of covenant faithfulness. The Teacher taught that loyalty to Jehovah required a complete and unwavering dedication to the Law, one that would not be influenced by external pressures or personal gain. His teachings presented a vision of faithfulness that was uncompromising, emphasizing that true worship could not coexist with the practices that the Wicked Priest had embraced.

In Deuteronomy 6:5, Jehovah commands, "You shall love Jehovah your God with all your heart and with all your soul and with all your might." The Teacher saw this command as central to the covenant, teaching his followers that their love for Jehovah must be reflected in their obedience to His commandments. This vision of covenant faithfulness served as a counter to the influence of the Wicked Priest, as it reminded the Qumran community that their loyalty to Jehovah required a complete rejection of any form of compromise.

The theological conflict between the Teacher and the Wicked Priest thus served as a defining feature of the Qumran community's identity. Through this conflict, the Teacher provided his followers with a clear understanding of what it meant to be faithful to Jehovah, emphasizing that true covenantal loyalty could not be reconciled with the practices of a corrupt priesthood. This vision of faithfulness gave the Qumran community a sense of purpose, as they saw themselves as a holy remnant, chosen to uphold Jehovah's Law in a world that had abandoned its commitment to righteousness.

CHAPTER 12 The Teacher of Righteousness and Messianic Expectations

Introduction: The Teacher's Influence on Qumran's Messianic Hopes

The Qumran community's anticipation of a Messiah—a deliverer chosen by Jehovah—reflects their profound hope for divine intervention amidst a period of perceived apostasy and corruption in Jerusalem. While the Teacher of Righteousness is not directly identified as the Messiah in the Qumran writings, his influence on the community's messianic expectations is evident. His teachings fostered a heightened sense of anticipation, encouraging his followers to look forward to a future figure who would fulfill Jehovah's promises of redemption and restoration. In a community that already saw itself as a remnant called to uphold divine standards, the Teacher of Righteousness inspired messianic hopes rooted in a vision of righteousness and covenant fidelity.

The Concept of the Messiah in Qumran Thought

In the Qumran community, the concept of a Messiah—or, in some texts, multiple messianic figures—represented a culmination of Jehovah's plan to restore Israel's purity and establish justice. This expectation was deeply intertwined with the community's view of themselves as a righteous remnant, awaiting vindication and the establishment of divine rule. The Teacher of Righteousness, through his teachings, shaped the contours of this messianic expectation, interpreting prophetic passages that pointed to a future deliverer who would embody the righteousness that the community revered.

The term "Messiah" derives from the Hebrew *Mashiach*, meaning "anointed one." In ancient Israel, the term was applied to kings, priests, and prophets who had been anointed to carry out Jehovah's purposes. For the Qumran community, however, the Messiah held a unique significance as one who would bring about the final, eschatological restoration. This hope finds resonance in passages like Isaiah 11:1, which promises, "There shall come forth a shoot from the stump of Jesse, and a branch from his roots shall bear fruit." The Teacher of Righteousness interpreted such passages as foretelling a divine figure who would lead the faithful remnant to triumph over their enemies.

The Teacher's Role as a Forerunner to the Messiah

The Qumran community saw the Teacher of Righteousness not as the Messiah himself, but as a precursor who prepared the way for the coming of the Messiah. His teachings emphasized the importance of righteousness, purity, and covenantal faithfulness, qualities that he believed would characterize the Messiah. In this sense, the Teacher served as a spiritual guide, setting the standard for the community's messianic expectations and instructing them on how to live in anticipation of the Messiah's arrival.

The Teacher's role as a forerunner can be compared to the way John the Baptist prepared the way for Jesus, as described in passages like Isaiah 40:3, which states, "A voice cries: 'In the wilderness prepare the way of Jehovah; make straight in the desert a highway for our God.'" While John the Baptist explicitly declared his role in preparing for the Messiah, the Teacher of Righteousness subtly set the framework for what the Qumran community expected in their deliverer. By emphasizing the importance of righteousness and purity, the Teacher oriented his followers towards a future in which these values would be embodied in their ultimate leader.

The Teacher's influence as a forerunner shaped the community's understanding of what the Messiah's role would entail. His teachings directed their attention toward the Messianic Age as a time of purification, judgment, and the vindication of Jehovah's faithful. The Teacher's example served as a standard against which the Messiah would be measured, reinforcing the community's expectation that their deliverer would be an exemplar of righteousness, guiding them to a new era of faithfulness to Jehovah's covenant.

Messianic Hope and the Promise of Redemption

The messianic expectations fostered by the Teacher of Righteousness centered around the promise of redemption and restoration. The Qumran community, isolated from the religious authorities in Jerusalem, looked to the Messiah as a figure who would rectify the injustices and spiritual corruption that had taken root in Israel. This hope of redemption is reflected in the Qumran texts, which depict the Messiah as a liberator who would deliver the community from oppression and establish a kingdom characterized by righteousness and justice.

The expectation of redemption finds its roots in the Hebrew Scriptures, where Jehovah repeatedly promises to deliver His people from their enemies and restore them to a place of blessing. In Isaiah 61:1-2, for example, the prophet declares, "The Spirit of Jehovah God is upon me, because Jehovah has anointed me to bring good news to the poor; he has sent me to bind up the brokenhearted, to proclaim liberty to the captives, and the opening of the prison to those who are bound; to proclaim the year of Jehovah's favor." The Teacher of Righteousness interpreted such passages as affirmations of the Messiah's role in bringing about the ultimate redemption of Jehovah's faithful remnant.

For the Qumran community, redemption was not merely a political or social deliverance but a spiritual restoration, a return to covenantal faithfulness and purity. The Teacher's teachings reinforced this vision, emphasizing that the Messiah would bring about a purification of Israel, ridding the community of those who had compromised the Law and leading the faithful into a new era of righteousness. This understanding of redemption was deeply tied to the community's identity, as they believed that they alone were prepared to receive the Messiah and to participate in the restoration of Jehovah's kingdom.

The Dual Messianic Expectation: Priestly and Royal Figures

One of the unique features of the Qumran community's messianic expectations is the belief in two Messiahs: one of a priestly nature and one of a royal nature. This dual messianic expectation reflects the community's desire for a leader who would address both the spiritual and political needs of Israel. The Teacher of Righteousness's influence can be seen in this dual expectation, as his teachings emphasized both the importance of priestly purity and the need for a righteous king to lead Israel.

The concept of two Messiahs aligns with the Qumran community's interpretation of passages like Zechariah 6:13, which states, "It is he who shall build the temple of Jehovah and shall bear royal honor, and shall sit and rule on his throne. And there shall be a priest on his throne, and the counsel of peace shall be between them both." The Teacher of Righteousness saw this verse as a prophecy of two distinct figures, each with a specific role in Jehovah's plan. The priestly Messiah would restore the purity of worship, while the royal Messiah would lead Israel in righteousness, establishing Jehovah's kingdom on earth.

This dual messianic expectation underscores the Teacher's belief in the importance of both spiritual and political leadership. By fostering this vision, the Teacher prepared his followers to anticipate a time when both the priesthood and the kingship would be restored to their rightful place under Jehovah's rule. This belief in two Messiahs also reinforced the Qumran community's sense of separation from the religious authorities in Jerusalem, as they believed that neither the current priesthood nor the monarchy reflected Jehovah's true intentions for His people.

The Messianic Age as a Time of Judgment and Restoration

The Qumran community's messianic expectations included a strong emphasis on judgment and the restoration of Israel. The

Teacher of Righteousness taught that the coming of the Messiah would signal the beginning of a time of reckoning, in which Jehovah would judge the wicked and vindicate the faithful. This belief was closely tied to the community's sense of themselves as a righteous remnant, set apart from a world that had largely abandoned Jehovah's commandments.

The theme of judgment in messianic expectation is rooted in passages like Isaiah 11:4, which declares, "But with righteousness he will judge the poor, and decide with fairness for the meek of the earth; and he will strike the earth with the rod of his mouth, and with the breath of his lips he will kill the wicked." The Teacher of Righteousness interpreted such passages as a promise that Jehovah's anointed one would bring justice to the faithful and destroy those who had turned away from the covenant. For the Qumran community, the coming of the Messiah was not only a time of hope but also a time of accountability, as they believed that the Messiah would purify Israel by removing the unfaithful and re-establishing a righteous order.

This expectation of judgment and restoration reinforced the Qumran community's commitment to purity and obedience. They believed that their separation from mainstream Judaism was a necessary step in preparing for the Messiah's arrival, as they sought to live in a way that would ensure their acceptance in the coming kingdom. The Teacher's teachings on judgment provided them with a clear understanding of what was required to remain in Jehovah's favor, as they anticipated a future in which their faithfulness would be rewarded and the wicked would face divine retribution.

The Teacher's Influence on the Community's Preparation for the Messiah

The Teacher of Righteousness played a critical role in preparing the Qumran community for the arrival of the Messiah. His teachings emphasized the importance of covenantal faithfulness, purity, and righteousness, qualities that he believed were essential for those who wished to participate in Jehovah's kingdom. Through his guidance, the Qumran community developed a rigorous standard of conduct, viewing their lifestyle as a means of demonstrating their commitment to Jehovah's covenant and their readiness to receive the Messiah.

This preparation is reflected in passages like Malachi 3:1-2, which states, "Behold, I send my messenger, and he will prepare the way before me. And Jehovah whom you seek will suddenly come to his temple; and the messenger of the covenant in whom you delight, behold, he is coming, says Jehovah of hosts. But who can endure the day of his coming, and who can stand when he appears?" The Teacher of Righteousness saw himself as fulfilling a similar role to this messenger, preparing the community for the coming of the Messiah by instructing them in the ways of righteousness and ensuring their adherence to Jehovah's commandments.

The Teacher's influence on the community's preparation for the Messiah extended beyond mere instruction; he created a comprehensive framework of beliefs and practices that defined what it meant to be faithful in anticipation of Jehovah's kingdom. His teachings provided the Qumran community with a clear sense of purpose, as they viewed their separation from the religious authorities in Jerusalem as a necessary part of their preparation for the Messiah's arrival. Through their adherence to the Teacher's standards, the Qumran community believed that they were preparing themselves to be a people worthy of Jehovah's deliverance.

The Messianic Legacy of the Teacher of Righteousness

The Teacher of Righteousness's influence on the Qumran community's messianic expectations cannot be overstated. Through his teachings, he shaped a vision of the Messiah as a figure who would embody righteousness, purity, and covenantal faithfulness, leading Israel into an era of judgment and restoration. The Teacher's role as a forerunner to the Messiah provided the Qumran community with a framework for understanding their place in Jehovah's plan, reinforcing their sense of identity as a faithful remnant and guiding them in their preparation for the coming kingdom.

The messianic expectations fostered by the Teacher of Righteousness remain a testament to the Qumran community's dedication to Jehovah and their unwavering hope for redemption. His teachings continue to provide insight into the community's beliefs, offering a glimpse into a world shaped by the hope of a future deliverer who would fulfill Jehovah's promises and restore Israel to a place of blessing and faithfulness.

Was Jesus Connected to the Essenes, or Are Their Teachings Irreconcilable with His?

The Essenes: Who Were They?

The Essenes were a Jewish sect that emerged during the second century B.C.E., around the time of the political and religious turmoil caused by the reign of Antiochus IV Epiphanes. This period, marked by the Seleucid oppression and desecration of the Jewish temple, prompted some Jewish groups to seek isolation and purity, viewing themselves as the true faithful in the midst of what they perceived as widespread apostasy within mainstream Judaism. This desire to maintain holiness and separation from the corruption of the world is what largely characterized the Essenes, as noted by historical sources such as Josephus (Jewish War, 2.8.2).

The name "Essene" may derive from the Hebrew term *Hasidim* (pious or loyal ones), reflecting their commitment to living according to strict interpretations of the Mosaic Law. They formed a secluded community near the Dead Sea, most likely in Qumran, where they devoted themselves to asceticism, communal living, and rigorous religious observances. Their community thrived until the second century C.E. when it dissolved after the Jewish-Roman wars.

In contrast to the more visible and politically active Pharisees and Sadducees, the Essenes distanced themselves from temple worship, rejecting animal sacrifices, likely due to their view of the temple priesthood as corrupt. Their focus was on spiritual purity, communal life, and awaiting the end of times, believing that they were living in an era of apostasy and judgment. The Essenes saw themselves as a remnant group awaiting the intervention of God to restore Israel.

Did Jesus Have Ties to the Essenes?

The speculation that Jesus had ties to the Essenes, or that He was influenced by their teachings, comes from certain similarities in their practices and locations. Both Jesus and John the Baptist spent time in the wilderness, and both preached a message of repentance and righteousness, calling for a return to godliness. However, these parallels do not substantiate the claim that Jesus was either an Essene or heavily influenced by this community.

The Essene hypothesis hinges on a series of assumptions, but it is important to critically evaluate the core distinctions between the teachings and mission of Jesus and those of the Essenes.

Silence on the Essenes: Does It Prove Affiliation?

One of the arguments presented by some proponents of the Essene connection is that Jesus never openly criticized the Essenes, while He did frequently confront the Pharisees and Sadducees. This silence, they argue, suggests that Jesus may have been sympathetic to the Essene way of life or was, perhaps, a part of their community.

However, this argument from silence is logically weak. The absence of any recorded criticism of the Essenes does not imply Jesus' approval or affiliation with them. The Gospels do not record Jesus commenting on every religious group or philosophy of His time. For instance, Jesus did not speak about various Greek philosophies or other religious groups in the Roman world, yet this silence does not imply His endorsement of them.

Moreover, the Essenes were not a significant part of mainstream Judaism, which might explain why they did not feature prominently in Jesus' public confrontations. The primary focus of His rebukes was the religious leaders (Pharisees and Sadducees) who held influence over the broader Jewish population, leading them astray with legalism and hypocrisy. As Jesus said in Matthew 23:13, "Woe to you, scribes and

Pharisees, hypocrites! For you shut the kingdom of heaven in people's faces. For you neither enter yourselves nor allow those who would enter to go in." His mission was to expose the spiritual blindness of those who wielded authority over the people, and the Essenes, as an isolated sect, were not part of this dynamic.

Major Differences Between Jesus' Teachings and Essene Doctrine

Despite some superficial similarities, the fundamental differences between the teachings of Jesus and the Essenes are stark. These distinctions reveal that Jesus could not have been part of the Essene community, nor could His mission be equated with theirs.

1. The Essenes Emphasized Legalism; Jesus Opposed It

The Essenes were known for their strict observance of the Mosaic Law, particularly in areas of ritual purity. Their legalism extended to radical practices such as abstinence from certain foods and other ascetic measures that they believed would maintain their spiritual purity. They were obsessed with ceremonial cleanliness, often going beyond the requirements of the Torah to ensure they remained undefiled.

In contrast, Jesus frequently opposed the kind of legalism that characterized not only the Pharisees but also the Essenes. Jesus taught that external rituals and strict adherence to the letter of the Law were not sufficient to achieve true righteousness. In Mark 7:15, Jesus declared, "There is nothing outside a person that by going into him can defile him, but the things that come out of a person are what defile him." This teaching directly opposed the Essenes' extreme focus on ritual purity and external observances.

Jesus emphasized the heart's condition rather than mere external conformity to religious rules. His rebukes against the Pharisees could easily apply to the Essenes, who also placed undue emphasis on outward observances while neglecting the more significant matters of mercy, justice, and love for others (Matthew 23:23).

2. Jesus Preached the Kingdom of God; The Essenes Did Not

One of the central themes of Jesus' ministry was the proclamation of the kingdom of God. Throughout the Gospels, Jesus emphasized that He had come to inaugurate God's reign, and He called people to repentance and faith in preparation for the kingdom. As He said in Matthew 4:17, "Repent, for the kingdom of heaven is at hand."

The Essenes, however, did not place the same emphasis on the kingdom of God. While they did believe in an apocalyptic end to history and awaited divine intervention, their focus was on withdrawing from society to live in isolation and asceticism. They believed that by separating themselves from the rest of Israel, they would preserve their purity in anticipation of God's judgment. Their hope was in the arrival of a messianic figure who would restore Israel, but they lacked the same proactive engagement with the world that characterized Jesus' ministry.

Jesus, on the other hand, brought the kingdom of God into the midst of the people, performing miracles, healing the sick, and teaching the masses about the love and mercy of God. His mission was not to withdraw from society but to seek and save the lost (Luke 19:10).

3. The Essenes Were Nationalists; Jesus Opened Salvation to All

The Essenes were intensely nationalistic in their outlook. They viewed themselves as the true remnant of Israel, and their community was closed to outsiders. Salvation, in their view, was reserved for those who belonged to the chosen people of Israel. They had no interest in Gentile inclusion and, like other Jewish sects, would have been hostile to the idea of opening the doors of salvation to non-Jews.

In stark contrast, Jesus' message of salvation was inclusive. He reached out to Gentiles and Samaritans, breaking the barriers that separated Jews from other nations. In John 4, Jesus' interaction with the Samaritan woman is a prime example of His openness to those outside the Jewish community. In Matthew 28:19-20, Jesus gave His disciples the Great Commission, commanding them to "make disciples of all nations."

Jesus' ministry made it clear that God's plan of salvation was for all people, Jew and Gentile alike. This inclusivity was a major point of divergence from the Essenes, who held to a narrow, nationalistic view of God's favor.

4. Jesus Taught About the Resurrection of the Body; The Essenes Did Not

Another critical difference between Jesus and the Essenes concerns the doctrine of resurrection. Jesus taught explicitly about the resurrection of the body. In John 11:25-26, Jesus proclaimed, "I am the resurrection and the life. Whoever believes in me, though he die, yet shall he live, and everyone who lives and believes in me shall never die."

The Essenes, on the other hand, did not place the same emphasis on bodily resurrection. Their beliefs tended more toward the immortality of the soul, with less focus on the restoration of the physical body. This distinction is vital because Jesus' resurrection from the dead is central to the Christian faith (1 Corinthians 15:14-17). His physical resurrection affirmed that the body itself would be raised, and this hope was offered to all who believe in Him. The Essenes did not share this same resurrection hope, as they focused more on spiritual purity and asceticism in this life rather than the hope of a bodily resurrection in the age to come.

Was Jesus the Essene "Teacher of Righteousness"?

Some scholars have suggested that Jesus was the Essene "Teacher of Righteousness," a figure mentioned in the Dead Sea Scrolls who played a leading role in the Essene community. However, this claim overlooks crucial theological and historical differences between Jesus and the Teacher of Righteousness.

While both figures taught about righteousness, the Essene leader was not the sinless Son of God. He was a priest in the Essene community, but Jesus' priesthood was of a different order entirely— "after the order of Melchizedek" (Hebrews 7:17). The Teacher of Righteousness needed purification for his sins, whereas Jesus was sinless, as 2 Corinthians 5:21 makes clear: "For our sake he made him to be sin who knew no sin, so that in him we might become the righteousness of God."

Additionally, the Teacher of Righteousness did not claim to be the Messiah, nor did he atone for the sins of others through his death. Jesus, on the other hand, was the promised Messiah, the Lamb of God who takes away the sin of the world (John 1:29). His death on the cross was a once-for-all sacrifice for sin, something the Essene leader could never claim. Furthermore, Jesus was resurrected from the dead, providing the ultimate proof of His divine identity and mission, whereas the Teacher of Righteousness died without being raised to life.

No Evidence of Essene Influence on Jesus

There is no compelling evidence that Jesus had any significant contact with the Essene community, nor is there any indication that their teachings shaped His ministry. While both groups emphasized righteousness, the differences between them are too significant to overlook. Jesus' identity as the Son of God, the Messiah, and the Savior of all humanity sets Him apart from any association with the Essenes.

Ultimately, Jesus came to fulfill the law and the prophets, bringing the kingdom of God to earth and opening the way of salvation to all who believe in Him (Matthew 5:17-18). His teachings, life, death, and resurrection stand in contrast to the legalism and isolationism of the Essenes, affirming that He was sent by God with a unique mission that transcended any particular Jewish sect or movement.

CHAPTER 13 Comparisons to Biblical Figures

Introduction: The Teacher of Righteousness in the Line of Prophetic Figures

The Teacher of Righteousness occupies a unique role within the Qumran community as both a guide and a source of divine insight, his influence anchored in a reverence for Jehovah's Law and a commitment to covenantal faithfulness. His life and mission bear significant resemblances to several key biblical figures, including Moses, Elijah, and John the Baptist. Each of these individuals played a role in Israel's history as restorers, reformers, and protectors of the Law. In examining these parallels, it becomes evident that the Teacher of Righteousness saw himself—and was seen by his community—as part of this lineage of prophetic leaders raised by Jehovah to guide His people back to righteousness.

Moses: A Lawgiver and Intermediary

One of the most profound connections the Qumran community drew between the Teacher of Righteousness and a biblical figure is that with Moses. As the preeminent lawgiver, Moses was Jehovah's chosen instrument for delivering Israel from Egyptian bondage and for receiving the Law at Sinai, which became the foundation of Israel's covenant with Jehovah (Exodus 20). Like Moses, the Teacher of Righteousness was viewed as a mediator between Jehovah and His people, bringing divine instruction and guidance to a community striving to maintain purity amid a world they perceived as corrupt.

The Role of the Law

Moses' role as a lawgiver is foundational to his identity, as seen in Exodus 24:12, where Jehovah tells him, "Come up to me on the mountain and wait there, that I may give you the tablets of stone, with the law and the commandment, which I have written for their instruction." This direct transmission of Jehovah's Law to Moses solidified his role as a custodian of divine truth. Similarly, the Teacher of Righteousness held a place of authority in the Qumran community, interpreting and teaching the Law in ways that set his followers apart from mainstream Judaism. He believed that the religious authorities in Jerusalem had strayed from the true Law, and his task was to preserve its purity for his followers.

The Teacher of Righteousness, like Moses, provided his community with interpretations of the Law that emphasized strict obedience and separation from corruption. His teachings insisted on an untainted observance of the covenant, a stance that resonates with the Deuteronomic calls for covenant faithfulness. Deuteronomy 6:17 admonishes, "You shall diligently keep the commandments of Jehovah your God, and his testimonies and his statutes, which he has commanded you." The Teacher echoed this call, positioning himself as a defender of the Law against those he perceived as apostates.

The Role of Mediator and Intercessor

Moses frequently acted as an intermediary for Israel, interceding on behalf of the people when they fell into sin. In Exodus 32:31-32, after the incident of the golden calf, Moses pleads with Jehovah, saying, "Alas, this people has sinned a great sin; they have made for themselves gods of gold. But now, if you will forgive their sin, but if not, please blot me out of your book that you have written." Moses' willingness to stand before Jehovah and seek forgiveness for Israel highlighted his commitment to his people's welfare and covenantal faithfulness.

The Teacher of Righteousness likewise took on the role of an intermediary, though in a different manner. His teachings emphasized the need for the Qumran community to maintain a distinct separation from the sinful practices of others. However, he did not simply call for isolation but instructed his followers in ways to uphold the covenant, thereby acting as a guide and a model of righteousness. Like Moses, he bore the responsibility of leading the community in faithfulness, standing between them and a world filled with impurity.

Elijah: A Prophet of Confrontation and Zeal for Jehovah

Elijah, known for his zealous defense of Jehovah's honor and his willingness to confront apostasy, provides another clear parallel to the Teacher of Righteousness. Elijah's ministry was marked by his relentless opposition to the idolatry promoted by King Ahab and Queen Jezebel, as recorded in 1 Kings 18. This unwavering commitment to Jehovah's commandments, even at great personal risk, mirrors the Teacher's own confrontations with those he deemed corrupt within the religious establishment.

Confrontation with Apostasy

Elijah's confrontation with the prophets of Baal on Mount Carmel stands as one of the most vivid examples of his prophetic role. In 1 Kings 18:21, Elijah challenges the people, saying, "How long will you go limping between two different opinions? If Jehovah is God, follow him; but if Baal, then follow him." This challenge was a call for Israel to reject idolatry and return to exclusive devotion to Jehovah. Elijah's willingness to stand alone against the prevailing religious corruption in Israel resonates with the Teacher of Righteousness's stance against the perceived apostasy of the Jerusalem priesthood.

The Teacher of Righteousness took a similarly bold stand, condemning the religious leaders in Jerusalem for abandoning the covenant. His criticisms of the "Wicked Priest" and other corrupt leaders bear a strong resemblance to Elijah's condemnation of Ahab and the prophets of Baal. The Teacher's message encouraged his community to see themselves as a faithful remnant, akin to Elijah's remnant of 7,000 who had not bowed to Baal (1 Kings 19:18). Like Elijah, the Teacher of Righteousness called for an uncompromising stance, one that refused to accommodate the sinful practices he saw in the religious establishment.

Zeal for Jehovah's Honor

Elijah's zeal for Jehovah's honor was evident in his willingness to confront sin directly, even when it placed him in danger. In 1 Kings 19:10, he states, "I have been very jealous for Jehovah, the God of hosts. For the people of Israel have forsaken your covenant, thrown down your altars, and killed your prophets with the sword, and I, even I only, am left." This expression of fervent dedication is mirrored in the Teacher of Righteousness's devotion to the purity of Jehovah's commandments.

The Teacher of Righteousness's teachings emphasize a similar zeal for Jehovah's holiness and an uncompromising stand against anything that would defile the covenant. This intensity, akin to Elijah's, served as a defining characteristic of the Qumran community's self-understanding. They saw themselves as uniquely devoted to Jehovah's service, untainted by the practices that had corrupted other groups within Judaism. The Teacher's message reinforced this identity, portraying the community as defenders of the covenant in a manner similar to Elijah's role as the defender of Jehovah's honor.

John the Baptist: A Voice Crying in the Wilderness

The comparison between the Teacher of Righteousness and John the Baptist rests upon their shared role as reformers and voices of repentance who lived in the wilderness, calling people to prepare for Jehovah's coming judgment. Both figures emphasized a return to purity and covenantal faithfulness, rejecting the prevailing religious practices that they viewed as compromising or corrupt.

The Call to Repentance

John the Baptist's ministry is marked by his call for repentance and preparation for Jehovah's coming kingdom. In Matthew 3:1-2, we read, "In those days John the Baptist came preaching in the wilderness of Judea, 'Repent, for the kingdom of heaven is at hand.'" This message of repentance, a turning away from sin and a return to covenant faithfulness, was central to John's role as the forerunner to Jesus.

Similarly, the Teacher of Righteousness called the Qumran community to a life of repentance and adherence to the covenant. His teachings focused on the need to separate from corrupt influences and maintain a life of purity, anticipating Jehovah's judgment upon those who had abandoned His commandments. Like John, the Teacher saw himself as preparing his followers for an impending divine reckoning, emphasizing that repentance and obedience were the means by which they would be preserved.

Life in the Wilderness and Separation from Society

Both John the Baptist and the Teacher of Righteousness chose lives of isolation in the wilderness as a means of separating themselves from the influences of a corrupt society. John's ministry in the wilderness reflected his commitment to purity, as he lived apart from the political and religious centers of his day. This separation underscored the seriousness of his message and his role as a prophetic voice calling Israel to repentance.

The Teacher of Righteousness led the Qumran community in a similar manner, establishing a society in the wilderness that was entirely separate from mainstream Judaism. This physical separation symbolized their spiritual dedication, reflecting a belief that true faithfulness required distance from the practices they viewed as impure. Just as John's wilderness ministry served as a critique of the religious establishment, the Teacher's establishment of a community in the Judean wilderness underscored his message of reform and the need for an unblemished devotion to Jehovah.

Preparing for Judgment

John the Baptist's role as a preparer of the way for Jesus included warnings of impending judgment, as seen in Matthew 3:10, where he says, "Even now the axe is laid to the root of the trees. Every tree therefore that does not bear good fruit is cut down and thrown into the fire." This message of judgment, coupled with his call to repentance, set the stage for Jesus' ministry and the establishment of Jehovah's kingdom.

The Teacher of Righteousness also prepared his followers for a time of judgment, emphasizing that their obedience to the covenant would protect them from divine wrath. He taught that the Qumran community represented a faithful remnant that would be preserved when Jehovah executed judgment upon the unfaithful. This eschatological focus, so central to the Teacher's teachings, closely mirrors John's emphasis on the need to bear "good fruit" as a demonstration of genuine faithfulness.

Conclusion: A Legacy of Faithfulness and Reform

The Teacher of Righteousness's life and mission bear striking resemblances to those of Moses, Elijah, and John the Baptist. Like Moses, he served as a lawgiver and mediator, guiding his followers in the ways of Jehovah's covenant. Like Elijah, he was zealous for Jehovah's honor, standing against apostasy and calling for an uncompromising faithfulness to Jehovah's commandments. And like John the Baptist, he called for repentance, establishing a community in the wilderness that would serve as a faithful remnant in anticipation of Jehovah's judgment.

Through these parallels, the Teacher of Righteousness positioned himself and his community within a lineage of prophetic figures who were dedicated to the defense and preservation of Jehovah's covenant. His teachings reinforced the Qumran community's identity as a chosen remnant, committed to upholding the Law and awaiting the fulfillment of Jehovah's promises. By examining these comparisons, one gains insight into the Qumran community's understanding of themselves as defenders of divine truth, shaped by the influence of a teacher who saw his role as part of a long line of faithful servants called to guide Jehovah's people.

CHAPTER 14 The Teacher's Influence on the Dead Sea Scrolls Community

Introduction: The Teacher's Role in Forging a Unique Community Identity

The Teacher of Righteousness significantly influenced the formation, beliefs, and practices of the Qumran community, an isolated group deeply committed to maintaining purity in doctrine and conduct. His guidance, teachings, and interpretation of the Law laid the foundation for a unique and resolute identity within Second Temple Judaism, setting the community apart in its dedication to Jehovah. Through a deep-seated sense of covenantal commitment, strict observance of the Law, and a shared vision of righteousness, the Teacher of Righteousness became both the spiritual cornerstone and prophetic voice of Qumran. His legacy within this community is woven through their writings, beliefs, and structure, which reflect his profound influence and lasting impact.

Establishing a Spiritual and Organizational Foundation

The Teacher of Righteousness did not merely contribute teachings; he was instrumental in shaping the very structure and organization of the Qumran community. His impact established the community as a distinct body with roles, regulations, and a communal way of life.

A Unique Hierarchy and Spiritual Leadership

The Teacher of Righteousness established a model of spiritual hierarchy intended to preserve purity and adherence to the Law within the community. Unlike mainstream Jewish sects such as the Pharisees or Sadducees, who sought influence within the temple system, the Teacher envisioned a separated community guided by a hierarchy that reinforced loyalty to Jehovah's commandments. This structure emphasized strict discipline and a clear chain of authority, with the Teacher positioned as both leader and interpreter of the divine will.

Key figures in the community, such as priests, overseers, and instructors, held authority to implement and uphold the teachings and regulations that the Teacher outlined. This community hierarchy mirrored aspects of the Levitical priesthood, as Jehovah had intended for His people, but with additional strictness. The members of the community who adhered closely to the Teacher's instruction were seen as fulfilling a sacred duty of upholding and preserving Jehovah's holy covenant.

The Community Rule: A Blueprint for Righteous Living

One of the most important documents reflecting the Teacher's influence is the Community Rule, which provides insight into the organization and ethical standards required within Qumran. This text contains regulations that governed every aspect of community life, including discipline, responsibilities, and spiritual practices. It is evident that the Teacher's teachings permeate the Community Rule, establishing a disciplined and obedient way of life that embodies the call to holiness and separation from the corrupted practices outside their fold.

The Community Rule outlines a process of initiation, confession, and commitment to a communal lifestyle centered on obedience to Jehovah. Each new member underwent a period of testing, underscoring the community's belief in a need for thorough spiritual and moral alignment with the Teacher's instruction. Through these practices, the Qumran community strove to embody Isaiah's call to be "a people of unclean lips" (Isaiah 6:5) made clean through Jehovah's guidance. This expectation of complete purity in behavior and belief reflected the Teacher's profound impact on their collective identity.

The Teacher's Doctrinal Influence and Interpretation of the Law

The Teacher of Righteousness imparted a distinctive interpretation of the Law that became central to the community's beliefs. His understanding emphasized a purity of faith, distinct from the religious authorities in Jerusalem, and his teachings reflected a belief that the existing temple practices had become contaminated.

A Purity Above the Rituals of the Jerusalem Temple

The Teacher of Righteousness taught that the temple and its leaders in Jerusalem had failed to uphold the sanctity of Jehovah's covenant, leading to an apostasy that necessitated separation. He believed that the Qumran community represented a faithful remnant, chosen to uphold true worship. In this context, the Teacher's interpretation of the Law demanded a strict, uncompromising observance beyond the rituals observed in Jerusalem.

This perspective can be compared with the prophet Ezekiel's critique of Israel's leadership, as seen in Ezekiel 22:26: "Her priests have done violence to my law and have profaned my holy things. They have made no distinction between the holy and the common, neither have they taught the difference between the unclean and the clean." The Teacher's teachings echoed this condemnation, viewing the established priesthood as spiritually compromised and encouraging the community to separate themselves as the true adherents of Jehovah's commands.

Interpretation of Key Prophetic Texts

The Teacher's teachings were deeply rooted in his interpretations of prophetic texts, which shaped the Qumran community's view of themselves as participants in an eschatological mission. The Teacher drew heavily on the prophecies of Isaiah, Jeremiah, and Habakkuk, aligning the Qumran community with the "faithful remnant" that these prophets foresaw in the face of apostasy.

In particular, the Habakkuk Commentary (1QpHab) exemplifies the Teacher's interpretation of prophecy, casting the Qumran community as the righteous who would be saved from judgment. Habakkuk 2:4, "the righteous shall live by his faith," became a foundational verse, applied to the community's pursuit of obedience. By framing the community within this prophetic vision, the Teacher emphasized their role as an elect group, chosen to uphold the Law even as they awaited Jehovah's intervention against their enemies.

The Role of Covenantal Faithfulness in Community Life

Central to the Teacher's influence was his emphasis on covenantal faithfulness, which he viewed as a sacred obligation that the community must uphold at all costs. The Teacher's interpretation of the covenant distinguished the Qumran community from other Jewish groups, as he believed they alone maintained the true covenant with Jehovah.

A Renewal of the Covenant

The Teacher saw the Qumran community as a restored covenant people, tasked with adhering strictly to Jehovah's commandments. This perspective resonated with the theme of covenant renewal found throughout Scripture, particularly in the writings of the prophets. In Jeremiah 31:31-33, Jehovah promises a new covenant with His people: "I will put my law within them, and I will write it on their hearts. And I will be their God, and they shall be my people." The Teacher interpreted this promise as applying to the Qumran community, who, through their adherence to the Law and separation from impurity, were fulfilling this prophecy.

The Teacher's teaching encouraged his followers to view their separation from mainstream Judaism as an expression of this covenantal renewal. Just as Israel had been called out from among the nations to be a people "holy to Jehovah" (Deuteronomy 7:6), so the Qumran community saw themselves as a chosen remnant, distinct and set apart.

A Daily Commitment to Righteousness

The Qumran community's daily practices were rooted in the Teacher's call to righteous living. Members committed to regular prayer, study, and communal meals as acts of devotion to Jehovah. These practices reflected a continuous dedication to the covenant, embodying the Teacher's teaching that their obedience must be unwavering.

Their lifestyle bore striking parallels to the instruction given in Psalm 1:1-2, which describes the blessed man as one who "walks not in the counsel of the wicked" but "meditates on his law day and night." The Teacher emphasized that this constant focus on righteousness was necessary for preserving their identity as a holy community. By continually renewing their commitment to the covenant, they were actively aligning themselves with Jehovah's will.

Eschatological Hope: The Teacher's Vision of Divine Deliverance

The Teacher of Righteousness instilled in the community a belief in Jehovah's impending judgment and the ultimate vindication of the righteous. His teachings conveyed a strong eschatological hope, envisioning a future in which Jehovah would intervene to rescue the faithful and punish the unfaithful.

Awaiting Divine Judgment

The Qumran community believed that Jehovah would soon judge the "sons of darkness" and deliver His faithful ones. This hope mirrored the Old Testament prophetic tradition, where Jehovah promises to judge the wicked and restore His faithful. For example, in Malachi 4:1-2, Jehovah says, "For behold, the day is coming, burning like an oven, when all the arrogant and all evildoers will be stubble…But for you who fear my name, the sun of righteousness shall rise with healing in its wings."

The Teacher's influence led the Qumran community to anticipate this day of judgment with a sense of urgency. They saw themselves as participants in Jehovah's plan, preparing for the coming judgment by living righteously. Their obedience and separation were seen not only as acts of faithfulness but as necessary preparation for the day when Jehovah would vindicate them.

The Community's Role in the Eschatological Plan

The Teacher of Righteousness taught that the Qumran community was instrumental in Jehovah's redemptive plan. Like the faithful remnant prophesied in Isaiah 10:21, "A remnant will return, the remnant of Jacob, to the mighty God," the Teacher positioned the

Qumran community as a group of faithful few who would remain loyal to Jehovah in the face of apostasy.

This understanding reinforced the community's commitment to their unique way of life. Their separation, strict observance of the Law, and communal solidarity were viewed as essential aspects of their identity as Jehovah's faithful remnant. Through the Teacher's influence, the Qumran community saw their existence as fulfilling a prophetic role within Jehovah's unfolding plan of redemption.

The Enduring Impact of the Teacher of Righteousness on Qumran's Identity

The Teacher of Righteousness was far more than a leader; he was the very source of the Qumran community's spiritual identity. His teachings, lifestyle, and interpretations of Scripture defined their beliefs, practices, and purpose. By emphasizing a distinct separation from the world, a strict adherence to the Law, and an expectation of Jehovah's coming judgment, the Teacher forged a community that saw themselves as a living testament to Jehovah's covenant.

Through his influence, the Qumran community believed they were upholding a divine standard that stood in opposition to the religious practices in Jerusalem, marking them as a remnant of true faith. Their commitment to this identity, rooted in the Teacher's teachings, sustained them through their years of isolation and solidified their understanding of themselves as Jehovah's chosen people.

CHAPTER 15 The Teacher of Righteousness and the New Testament

Introduction: Exploring the Links Between the Teacher of Righteousness and New Testament Teachings

The Teacher of Righteousness profoundly influenced his followers within the Qumran community, shaping their understanding of righteousness, prophecy, and devotion to Jehovah's Law. Comparisons between the Teacher's impact on the Qumran sect and the broader spiritual themes found within the New Testament have sparked much discussion. Given that both the Qumran community and early Christians sought a life aligned with the Scriptures, a natural question arises regarding the Teacher of Righteousness's relationship to the New Testament, particularly in light of common themes like faithfulness, divine judgment, and the expectation of a coming deliverance.

It is essential to approach this chapter with a clear understanding that any parallels observed between the Teacher of Righteousness and New Testament teachings are based on thematic similarities rather than any claim of influence. The New Testament records teachings directly from Jesus and his apostles, while the Dead Sea Scrolls reflect the unique and isolated beliefs of the Qumran community. Nevertheless, by examining these thematic connections, we can gain a clearer understanding of the distinctions and points of comparison that shed light on both the Teacher's role and the biblical narrative of the New Testament.

Common Themes of Righteousness and Purity: The Teacher of Righteousness and New Testament Teachings

The theme of righteousness occupies a central position in both the teachings of the Teacher of Righteousness and the New Testament. While both sources emphasize purity, holiness, and an unyielding dedication to Jehovah, their interpretations and applications reveal distinct approaches to attaining these virtues.

Righteousness in the Qumran Community's Doctrine

The Teacher of Righteousness held that his followers constituted a righteous remnant, chosen to uphold Jehovah's Law despite the corruption of mainstream religious authorities in Jerusalem. His call for separation from what he saw as apostate practices underscored his commitment to purity and a rigorous observance of the Law, which he saw as necessary for remaining in Jehovah's favor. This perspective is reflected in the Qumran community's lifestyle, characterized by strict adherence to rituals of purity, frequent immersion in ritual baths, and a dedication to preserving doctrinal purity in all aspects of community life.

In a similar vein, Paul in Romans 3:21-22 addresses the righteousness that comes "through faith in Jesus Christ to all who believe," marking a shift from strict adherence to the Law alone to a faith that embodies Jehovah's righteousness. However, the New Testament presents righteousness as attainable through faith in Jesus, while the Teacher of Righteousness taught a strict, legalistic path to purity that relied on obedience to the Law without a central figure like Jesus who provides grace.

The New Testament's Approach to Purity and Righteousness

In the New Testament, purity and righteousness are central tenets of Christian faith but are expressed within the framework of grace, forgiveness, and faith in Jesus as the Messiah. The Qumran community's strict adherence to ritual purity contrasts with the New Testament teaching that inner purity begins with a heart transformed by faith in Christ. Jesus taught, "Blessed are the pure in heart, for they shall see God" (Matthew 5:8), emphasizing that purity is not merely a matter of ritual but a quality of the heart that aligns one's life with Jehovah's commandments.

Moreover, in Matthew 23:25-28, Jesus rebukes the Pharisees for their focus on outward purity while neglecting inner righteousness, teaching that it is the heart's condition that defines true purity before Jehovah. In contrast, the Teacher's teachings imply that outward observance played a significant role in defining righteousness. The Qumran community's practice, guided by the Teacher, was one of separation and ritual purity. The New Testament's emphasis on internal transformation, however, calls for believers to "cleanse ourselves from all defilement of flesh and spirit" (2 Corinthians 7:1), stressing spiritual purity over ritual.

Eschatological Expectation and Judgment: The Teacher's Vision and New Testament Hope

A strong sense of eschatological hope and impending judgment permeates both the writings attributed to the Teacher of Righteousness and the teachings of the New Testament. Both sources envision a time when Jehovah will judge the unfaithful and reward the righteous, but they differ in how they present the unfolding of this divine plan.

The Teacher's Eschatological Vision of a Divine Judgment

The Teacher of Righteousness instructed the Qumran community to prepare for a coming day of judgment in which Jehovah would destroy the "sons of darkness," vindicating the "sons of light." This language is explicit in the War Scroll (1QM), which delineates the conflict between these two groups, reflecting the Qumran community's belief that they would play a role in Jehovah's judgment against apostasy. The community saw itself as a faithful remnant awaiting divine intervention, and they anticipated a messianic figure who would lead them to victory over their enemies.

This eschatological expectation is consistent with Old Testament prophecies, such as Isaiah 11:4, which describes the Messianic figure who will "strike the earth with the rod of his mouth, and with the breath of his lips he shall slay the wicked." The Qumran community saw themselves in alignment with such prophetic visions, and the Teacher's emphasis on coming judgment underscored the need for their strict separation from those they viewed as unrighteous.

New Testament Teachings on Judgment and Deliverance

The New Testament also presents a message of impending judgment and deliverance but with a distinct focus on Jesus as the fulfillment of Jehovah's promises. Jesus repeatedly warns of coming judgment, stating that Jehovah's wrath will fall upon the unrepentant. In Matthew 24, Jesus describes the tribulations that will precede his return, an event accompanied by "the Son of Man coming on the clouds of heaven with power and great glory" (Matthew 24:30). Unlike the Teacher of Righteousness, however, Jesus presents himself as the very means by which believers are spared from judgment.

Moreover, Paul emphasizes the deliverance available through Jesus, proclaiming in 1 Thessalonians 1:10 that Jesus "delivers us from the wrath to come." This sense of deliverance stands in contrast to the Teacher's teachings, where salvation is achieved through rigorous observance of the Law rather than through reliance on a Messianic Redeemer. The New Testament promises believers a place in Jehovah's kingdom through faith in Jesus Christ, while the Qumran community held that only through strict adherence to the Teacher's doctrines would they be delivered from the wrath to come.

The Role of the Teacher of Righteousness and the Role of Jesus: Prophet, Priest, and Leader

Both the Teacher of Righteousness and Jesus served as central figures who provided spiritual guidance, taught doctrines, and upheld a distinct interpretation of Jehovah's Law. However, their roles and self-understandings diverge significantly, particularly in light of Jesus' claims of divine authority and the Teacher's more limited role as an interpreter and guardian of the Law.

The Teacher as a Prophetic Figure and Interpreter

The Teacher of Righteousness, seen as a prophet and spiritual leader, guided the Qumran community in its pursuit of purity and covenantal faithfulness. His primary role was to interpret the Law and the Prophets, providing his followers with a clear path to righteousness through detailed guidance and correction. He served as a human mediator, applying Jehovah's Law to the community's everyday practices and calling them to a strict observance that would shield them from divine judgment.

Unlike Jesus, who declared himself to be "the way, and the truth, and the life" (John 14:6), the Teacher did not present himself as a unique path to Jehovah. Instead, he saw himself as a guardian of the Law, tasked with preserving its integrity. He warned against the practices of Jerusalem's religious leaders but did not claim to replace the temple or the sacrifices.

Jesus as the Fulfillment of Prophecy and the Way to Jehovah

In contrast, Jesus presented himself as the fulfillment of the Law and the Prophets, identifying himself as the long-awaited Messiah who would bring salvation to both Jews and Gentiles. In Matthew 5:17, he declared, "Do not think that I have come to abolish the Law or the Prophets; I have not come to abolish them but to fulfill them." Through this statement, Jesus asserted a role that transcended that of an interpreter; he positioned himself as the one who embodied and completed Jehovah's plan for humanity.

Jesus' unique role as both High Priest and the ultimate sacrifice for sin stands in stark contrast to the Teacher's leadership. As Hebrews 7:26-27 states, "For it was indeed fitting that we should have such a high priest, holy, innocent, unstained, separated from sinners, and exalted above the heavens…he did this once for all when he offered up himself." Unlike the Teacher of Righteousness, who did not claim divine authority over salvation, Jesus offered himself as the path to eternal life and reconciliation with Jehovah, a claim that surpassed any similar role among the Jewish sects, including the Qumran community.

Distinct Approaches to Community and Mission

Both the Qumran community and the early Christian church emphasized communal life and a shared commitment to Jehovah's principles. However, their missions and goals diverged, reflecting the difference between the Teacher's instruction and the mission given by Jesus to his followers.

The Qumran Community's Mission of Separation and Purity

The Qumran community, guided by the Teacher of Righteousness, sought separation from the religious corruption they perceived in the larger Jewish world, isolating themselves in a desert commune dedicated to purity and obedience to Jehovah's commandments. Their mission was not evangelical; rather, they viewed themselves as a remnant who would be vindicated by Jehovah's judgment upon the impure and unfaithful.

The Christian Mission of Evangelism and Discipleship

Jesus, however, directed his disciples to go "into all the world and proclaim the gospel to the whole creation" (Mark 16:15). The New Testament church embraced a mission of outreach, evangelism, and discipleship, seeking to bring all nations into fellowship with Jehovah. Unlike the Qumran community, the Christian church was called to interact with the world rather than withdraw from it, living as "salt of the earth" and "light of the world" (Matthew 5:13-14).

This contrast highlights a foundational difference between the Teacher's emphasis on separation and Jesus' call for his followers to engage with the world, spreading the message of salvation. While the Teacher's followers sought righteousness by isolation, Jesus' followers were commanded to make disciples of all nations, embodying Jehovah's love through their actions and words.

CHAPTER 16 The Teacher's Legacy: From Qumran to Modern Scholarship

Introduction: Defining the Teacher's Lasting Legacy

The Teacher of Righteousness, a prominent leader of the Qumran community, remains a significant figure in the Dead Sea Scrolls and has sparked extensive scholarly investigation in modern biblical studies. His influence within Qumran is evident through his doctrinal teachings, interpretative methods, and the organizational structure he established for a group deeply devoted to Jehovah and the pursuit of purity. While much about his life and identity is shrouded in mystery, the Teacher's legacy within the Qumran sect and broader Jewish history is unmistakable. In recent decades, this legacy has expanded beyond Qumran, as scholars continue to explore his writings and consider the Teacher's influence on early Jewish thought, providing valuable insights into understanding ancient Judaism and biblical interpretation.

The Teacher's Role in Establishing Qumran Ideology and Practices

The Teacher of Righteousness was more than a mere figurehead for the Qumran community; he was a pivotal influence in shaping its religious ideology, communal practices, and the community's distinct separation from the religious establishment in Jerusalem. His emphasis on purity, separation from what he deemed corrupt influences, and a strict adherence to the Law solidified his legacy within the Qumran sect.

The Teacher's Doctrinal Teachings

Central to the Teacher's legacy are his doctrinal contributions, which highlight his interpretations of Jewish Law and his prophetic insights. Known for his commitment to the Law of Moses, he established a strict legal code within the community, marked by unique interpretations of purity, Sabbath observance, and dietary restrictions. His teachings reinforced the Qumran community's role as a righteous remnant, a group isolated to preserve their faith in Jehovah amidst what he saw as widespread apostasy.

In the Damascus Document, the Teacher lays out a vision for a covenantal community that adheres to Jehovah's commands with an unparalleled level of commitment. His emphasis on the covenant reflects the teachings in Deuteronomy 30:16, which reminds the faithful, "If you obey the commandments of Jehovah your God that I command you today, by loving Jehovah your God, by walking in his ways, and by keeping his commandments and his statutes and his rules, then you shall live and multiply." The Teacher urged his followers to maintain this covenant through obedience, considering themselves set apart from those who had deviated from the Law.

Developing Qumran's Ritual and Community Practices

Under the Teacher's guidance, the Qumran community adopted rigorous ritual practices that emphasized purity and piety. These rituals included frequent purification ceremonies, daily prayers, and communal meals that symbolized their unity in faith. The Manual of Discipline (1QS), one of the foundational texts of the community, outlines these practices, detailing the protocols for initiating new members, maintaining spiritual cleanliness, and the penalties for transgressions within the group. The Teacher's strict adherence to these practices reinforced his followers' commitment to living as a holy remnant, setting them apart from mainstream Judaism.

In a similar vein, the Qumran community's interpretation of sacrificial rites and offerings underscored their belief that they represented the true Israel. Although they abstained from sacrifices in the temple, the community considered their lifestyle of devotion and purity as a spiritual offering. Psalm 51:17 reflects this sentiment, saying, "The sacrifices of God are a broken spirit; a broken and contrite heart, O God, you will not despise." By encouraging a life of righteousness, the Teacher positioned his followers to honor Jehovah through obedience and reverence, maintaining their sanctity through moral and ritual purity.

The Teacher's Prophetic Legacy and Messianic Vision

One of the defining aspects of the Teacher's legacy is his eschatological outlook, which fostered a sense of prophetic mission within the Qumran community. His teachings emphasized a divine plan in which Jehovah would bring justice to the faithful remnant while judging those who had strayed from righteousness. This belief in Jehovah's impending judgment contributed to the Qumran community's resolve to remain pure, even in isolation.

Anticipating Divine Judgment and Vindication

The Teacher's prophetic insights shaped the Qumran community's eschatological worldview. His conviction that Jehovah would soon intervene and judge both Israel and the nations influenced the community's practices and set them on a path of waiting for divine vindication. The War Scroll (1QM) presents this anticipation of a final battle between the "sons of light" and the "sons of darkness," encapsulating the community's belief in Jehovah's coming judgment.

Scripture supports this eschatological outlook, as seen in Zephaniah 1:14, "The great day of Jehovah is near, near and hastening fast; the sound of the day of Jehovah is bitter; the mighty man cries aloud there." The Teacher's encouragement to remain steadfast in righteousness and obedience is rooted in the hope that Jehovah would soon bring justice. His teachings emphasized that the faithful would ultimately be vindicated, motivating the community to maintain their covenantal purity.

The Teacher's Messianic Expectations

The Teacher of Righteousness also left a legacy of Messianic hope, as he believed Jehovah would raise a messianic figure to deliver and restore the faithful. Although the Teacher did not claim the title of Messiah for himself, he anticipated that Jehovah would send a deliverer who would lead the righteous in the final judgment. This expectation aligns with prophecies such as Isaiah 11:4, which describes a messianic figure who "shall strike the earth with the rod of his mouth, and with the breath of his lips he shall kill the wicked."

This Messianic vision sustained the Qumran community's faith, as they awaited divine intervention and the restoration of Israel. The Teacher's legacy of Messianic expectation became integral to the community's worldview, shaping their understanding of divine justice and the coming kingdom.

Influence of the Teacher's Writings on Modern Biblical Scholarship

The discovery of the Dead Sea Scrolls has led to a significant re-evaluation of Jewish history, religious practices, and scriptural interpretation. Modern scholarship has gained valuable insights into the diversity of Second Temple Judaism, much of which is attributed to the Teacher's teachings. The Teacher's writings, preserved in texts such as the Damascus Document and the Habakkuk Commentary, provide a unique perspective on Jewish law, eschatology, and community organization that continues to enrich contemporary biblical studies.

Contributions to Understanding Second Temple Judaism

The Teacher's writings have broadened our understanding of Second Temple Judaism, revealing the range of religious practices within Jewish life during this period. His emphasis on strict observance of the Law and community separation illustrates the wide spectrum of belief and practice among Jewish groups. This variety contrasts with the commonly held view of Second Temple Judaism as a monolithic entity and underscores the extent to which different Jewish sects, including the Qumran community, interpreted and practiced the Law in distinct ways.

Enhancing Textual Studies and Interpretation of the Old Testament

Modern scholars studying the Teacher's commentaries, especially the Habakkuk Commentary (1QpHab), have gained insights into the exegetical methods employed within the Qumran community. The

Teacher's approach to Scripture reveals a literalist method of interpretation, in which prophecies are seen as having imminent fulfillment in the Teacher's own time. For instance, the Teacher's interpretation of Habakkuk 2:4 in the Commentary aligns with his belief in divine justice, suggesting that "the righteous shall live by his faith," is fulfilled in the faithful remnant at Qumran.

This literal approach contrasts with later allegorical interpretations that emerged within Hellenistic thought. The Teacher's straightforward interpretation has influenced modern scholarship by underscoring the importance of literal exegesis within certain Jewish sects, informing debates on Old Testament interpretation.

The Teacher's Enduring Legacy on Religious Communities and Beliefs

The Teacher of Righteousness's legacy endures within modern religious communities and academic discourse, as his teachings provide a model of devout living in accordance with Jehovah's Law. His emphasis on covenantal faithfulness and separation from worldly influence resonates with those seeking to maintain spiritual purity.

Inspiration for Religious Devotion and Purity

The Teacher's insistence on a lifestyle of purity and devotion has inspired many within religious communities to pursue lives that align closely with Scripture. His example serves as a reminder of the importance of upholding Jehovah's commandments and living in opposition to prevailing cultural or religious trends. Much like the Teacher's community at Qumran, modern groups dedicated to scriptural faithfulness view their commitment as a response to a world that often contradicts Jehovah's commands.

Ongoing Interest in Eschatological Beliefs

The Teacher's eschatological perspective and Messianic hope have also impacted modern eschatological beliefs, particularly in understanding the diversity of apocalyptic expectations in ancient Judaism. His emphasis on divine judgment and the ultimate vindication of the faithful continues to inform discussions on prophetic literature and eschatology. This interest in apocalypticism highlights the relevance of the Teacher's teachings for those who view the Bible as a prophetic revelation of Jehovah's coming kingdom.

Conclusion: The Teacher's Enduring Influence in Scholarship and Faith

The Teacher of Righteousness has left an indelible mark on both his community and modern biblical scholarship. His teachings on righteousness, separation, and adherence to Jehovah's Law shaped the Qumran community's practices and beliefs, creating a legacy that endures in the modern study of the Dead Sea Scrolls. The Teacher's writings have enriched our understanding of Second Temple Judaism and have provided scholars with a deeper appreciation for the range of Jewish belief in the centuries leading up to the New Testament. His legacy continues to inspire those who seek to remain faithful to Jehovah's commands, and his teachings remain a source of reflection for those who study the profound intersection between scripture, history, and faith.

CHAPTER 17 The Teacher of Righteousness and Apocalypticism

The Teacher of Righteousness and the Roots of Apocalypticism

The Teacher of Righteousness is not merely a figure within the Qumran sect but stands as a pivotal voice in apocalyptic thought that permeated Jewish beliefs during the Second Temple period. In an era marked by oppression and spiritual turmoil, the Teacher's doctrines and visions significantly contributed to the Qumran community's understanding of divine intervention, end-times judgment, and the vindication of the faithful. His teachings, preserved within the Dead Sea Scrolls, particularly the Damascus Document, the War Scroll, and the Commentary on Habakkuk, reveal a profound expectation of Jehovah's judgment on the wicked and deliverance of the righteous.

The Teacher's apocalyptic vision centered on the imminent intervention of Jehovah to establish justice. He saw his community, often referred to as the "sons of light," as participants in a cosmic struggle between good and evil, a battle that would culminate in divine judgment. The Teacher's influence on apocalyptic literature is paramount, as his understanding of prophecy, righteousness, and judgment reflects a worldview that anticipated Jehovah's direct role in human affairs, bringing ultimate resolution to spiritual conflict. This theme of divine intervention aligns with Old Testament prophecies, such as Isaiah 13:11, which states, "I will punish the world for its evil, and the wicked for their iniquity; I will put an end to the pomp of the arrogant and lay low the pompous pride of the ruthless."

The Concept of Dualism in the Teacher's Apocalyptic Thought

One of the defining features of the Teacher's apocalyptic vision is a pronounced dualism, an understanding of the world as divided between forces of good and evil, light and darkness. This dualistic worldview underpins the Qumran community's separation from mainstream Jewish society and their self-identification as the "sons of light." The Teacher believed that his followers were called to stand apart from a world enmeshed in corruption and apostasy, awaiting Jehovah's judgment on the "sons of darkness." This division is not merely symbolic but reflects a tangible struggle, one that would be realized in the eschatological war depicted in the War Scroll.

The Teacher's approach to dualism draws from scriptural foundations. Proverbs 4:18-19 offers a thematic parallel: "But the path of the righteous is like the light of dawn, which shines brighter and brighter until full day. The way of the wicked is like deep darkness; they do not know over what they stumble." In this passage, light and darkness are not simply metaphors but represent diverging paths of obedience to Jehovah versus rebellion. The Teacher's understanding of dualism was not philosophical but firmly rooted in moral obedience and covenantal faithfulness. For him, the path of light represented adherence to divine law, while darkness symbolized a rejection of Jehovah's covenant, an outlook that strongly shaped the community's identity and eschatological hope.

Prophetic Insight and the End of Days: The Teacher's Eschatological Role

The Teacher's role within the Qumran community went beyond that of a mere interpreter of the Law; he was perceived as a prophet with divine insight into the mysteries of the end times. The Commentary on Habakkuk illustrates his belief in a near-future intervention by Jehovah, who would execute judgment against the wicked and restore the faithful remnant. The Teacher's eschatology carried a tone of urgency and anticipation, urging his followers to remain steadfast amidst trials, for Jehovah's vindication was imminent.

Isaiah 11:4 reflects this hope in Jehovah's righteous judgment, stating, "But with righteousness he will judge the poor, and decide with fairness for the meek of the earth; and he will strike the earth with the rod of his mouth, and with the breath of his lips he will kill the wicked." The Teacher's prophetic vision resonates with this assurance of divine justice, encouraging the community to await Jehovah's intervention as the ultimate solution to the world's corruption and apostasy.

In his interpretation of biblical prophecy, the Teacher exemplified a literal approach, seeing the events foretold in books such as Habakkuk as speaking directly to the experiences of his time. His exegesis not only gave immediate relevance to ancient texts but also reinforced the belief that the Qumran community lived on the threshold of Jehovah's judgment. This apocalyptic fervor influenced the community's day-to-day life, as they viewed themselves as participants in Jehovah's prophetic plan, called to uphold righteousness as they awaited divine intervention.

The War Scroll: Defining the Cosmic Conflict

The War Scroll (1QM) is one of the primary texts that captures the Teacher's apocalyptic vision, portraying an ultimate battle between the sons of light and the sons of darkness. This document outlines a vivid eschatological scenario in which the Qumran community, as the chosen of Jehovah, is destined to engage in a final, decisive conflict. This battle is depicted not only as a physical confrontation but as a spiritual struggle between the forces of righteousness and evil, reflecting the Teacher's belief in the cosmic scale of this conflict.

The War Scroll specifies the roles, strategies, and even the priestly blessings that will accompany the sons of light into battle. This organized approach to the final conflict reflects the Teacher's conviction that Jehovah's chosen people would actively participate in His judgment. Revelation 19:11-14 echoes a similar vision of divine judgment, "Then I saw heaven opened, and behold, a white horse! The one sitting on it is called Faithful and True, and in righteousness he judges and makes war... And the armies of heaven, arrayed in fine linen, white and pure, were following him on white horses."

The Teacher's insistence on ritual purity and moral righteousness aligns with the War Scroll's emphasis on a sanctified people prepared for divine warfare. By establishing this cosmic conflict, the Teacher further solidified the community's identity, uniting them under a common purpose and preparing them for the day of Jehovah's judgment.

Ethical Vigilance and Purity: The Teacher's Command for Readiness

The Teacher's apocalyptic vision was deeply intertwined with his ethical and ritual expectations. He called for an unwavering commitment to purity, as he believed only those wholly devoted to Jehovah's covenant could withstand the impending divine judgment. His teachings emphasized moral vigilance, urging the community to avoid anything that might defile their spiritual standing. For the Teacher, apocalyptic readiness required an adherence to the Law that went beyond mere observance, demanding a lifestyle marked by sanctity and unwavering dedication.

This call to ethical vigilance is echoed in passages such as Isaiah 35:8, "And a highway shall be there, and it shall be called the Way of Holiness; the unclean shall not pass over it. It shall belong to those who walk on the way; even if they are fools, they shall not go astray." The Teacher's insistence on purity mirrored this vision of a path of holiness, a requirement for those who awaited Jehovah's intervention. For the Qumran community, spiritual vigilance became a defining feature, distinguishing them as the faithful remnant who stood ready for Jehovah's judgment.

The Teacher's Legacy in Apocalyptic Thought

The Teacher of Righteousness left an enduring legacy on apocalyptic thought within Second Temple Judaism and, by extension, on the development of eschatological themes in later Jewish and Christian texts. His teachings offered a structured worldview that interpreted historical events as markers of divine prophecy, fostering a mindset that saw current struggles as preludes to Jehovah's judgment.

This framework of thought provided a foundation for understanding subsequent apocalyptic literature, particularly as it relates to the ultimate triumph of good over evil.

The Teacher's influence is reflected in later Jewish apocalyptic works, as well as in the New Testament, where the theme of divine judgment and the vindication of the righteous plays a central role. Passages such as Matthew 13:41-43, in which Jesus speaks of the separation of the righteous from the wicked at the end of the age, carry echoes of the Teacher's apocalyptic vision: "The Son of Man will send his angels, and they will gather out of his kingdom all causes of sin and all law-breakers, and throw them into the fiery furnace. In that place, there will be weeping and gnashing of teeth. Then the righteous will shine like the sun in the kingdom of their Father."

Through his teachings, the Teacher of Righteousness established a lasting contribution to apocalyptic thought, presenting a vision of a world restored through divine judgment and the establishment of righteousness. His apocalyptic expectations remain a compelling testimony to his belief in Jehovah's sovereignty and the ultimate redemption of the faithful.

Conclusion: The Teacher's Apocalyptic Vision as a Testament to His Faith

The Teacher of Righteousness' apocalyptic vision has not only shaped the Qumran community but also contributed to the broader framework of eschatological thought within biblical tradition. His emphasis on the imminent intervention of Jehovah, the sanctity of the righteous, and the ultimate triumph of light over darkness is a profound testament to his faith and conviction. Through his teachings, the Teacher offered his community hope and guidance, calling them to remain steadfast in obedience as they awaited Jehovah's intervention and the fulfillment of His promises. The Teacher's legacy endures as a powerful reminder of the hope that lies at the heart of apocalyptic faith—a hope rooted in the assurance of divine justice and the establishment of Jehovah's eternal kingdom.

CHAPTER 18 The Ethics of Righteousness: Lessons from the Teacher

Introduction: Ethics and Righteousness in the Teachings of the Teacher

The figure known as the Teacher of Righteousness holds a pivotal place within the Dead Sea Scrolls, providing a framework for ethics that emphasizes a life wholly committed to God's commandments. His instructions and exhortations within the Scrolls reflect a rigorous commitment to righteousness, viewing ethical living as not merely an individual endeavor but an obligation for the community that aligns itself under Jehovah's sovereignty. Central to his teachings is a call to separate from the "sons of darkness" and adhere to a lifestyle of purity and obedience. Through understanding the ethics outlined by the Teacher, we can grasp the values and expectations he established for those in the Qumran community, which exemplifies an unwavering dedication to righteousness, seen as both a spiritual pursuit and a practical daily application.

The Call to Holiness: Separation from Iniquity

The Teacher's ethical framework places strong emphasis on separation from worldly influences. This separation, which characterizes the Qumran community, aligns with the biblical understanding that God's people are called to be distinct. In Leviticus 20:26, Jehovah declares, "You shall be holy to me, for I am Jehovah who sanctifies you." This foundational principle resonates with the Teacher's directives, as he urges his followers to reject the influences of those who walk contrary to God's ways.

This separation goes beyond mere physical distance; it is a moral and spiritual distancing from practices that lead away from God's commandments. The Teacher's writings demonstrate a strong concern that even slight associations with unrighteous behavior can corrupt the faithful. Echoing the sentiment found in Proverbs 4:14-15, "Do not enter the path of the wicked, and do not walk in the way of the evil. Avoid it; do not go on it," the Teacher admonishes the community to remain steadfast in their resolve against any form of compromise with unrighteousness.

Obedience to God's Commandments: The Foundation of Righteous Living

In the teachings of the Teacher of Righteousness, obedience to God's commandments is central. This obedience is not viewed as a burdensome requirement but as the very essence of righteousness. He sees adherence to God's laws as an act of devotion, demonstrating commitment to God's authority. The Teacher's instructions often echo Deuteronomy 6:5-6, which states, "You shall love Jehovah your God with all your heart and with all your soul and with all your might. And these words that I command you today shall be on your heart."

The Teacher's emphasis on obedience reflects a worldview that places God's law at the core of ethical living. His writings frequently portray disobedience as an act of rebellion, equating a disregard for God's law with alignment with the forces of darkness. This ethical standpoint reinforces the Teacher's perception of the world as a battlefield between righteousness and wickedness. By obeying God's commands, the followers of the Teacher are seen as participating in a divine mandate to establish a realm of holiness amidst a world of moral decay.

Justice and Fairness: Treating One Another Righteously

The ethics of the Teacher extend beyond individual righteousness to encompass the treatment of others within the community. In his teachings, he emphasizes justice and fair dealings, viewing them as critical components of righteous living. This emphasis is consistent with the biblical call to "do justice, and to love kindness, and to walk humbly with your God" (Micah 6:8). Justice, according to the Teacher, is not merely an abstract ideal but a practical expectation in interactions within the community.

The Dead Sea Scrolls reveal that the Teacher placed considerable importance on equitable treatment, rebuking any forms of deceit, slander, or oppression. His instructions imply that righteousness must permeate all aspects of life, especially in dealings with fellow members of the community. This focus on justice underscores the community's identity as a place of refuge from the corruption present in the broader society. The Teacher's stance is that justice within the community mirrors the justice of God, setting an example of integrity and fairness that aligns with Jehovah's commandments.

Humility and the Rejection of Pride

Humility is a recurring theme in the Teacher's ethical teachings, echoing the Scriptural admonition that "pride goes before destruction, and a haughty spirit before a fall" (Proverbs 16:18). The Teacher regards pride as a dangerous obstacle to righteousness, fostering a spirit that opposes submission to God's authority. In the Qumran community, humility is a virtue essential to maintaining unity and deference to divine instruction. The Teacher's disdain for pride is evident in his warnings against arrogance, which he sees as a threat to both personal and communal holiness.

The emphasis on humility aligns with the ethical teachings in passages such as James 4:6, which states, "God opposes the proud but gives grace to the humble." The Teacher's writings imply that those who seek personal glory are in direct conflict with the community's mission to honor Jehovah above all else. By promoting humility, the Teacher reinforces a mindset of servitude and dedication to God's will, encouraging the members of the community to view themselves as servants in the greater work of righteousness.

The Role of Discipline and Correction

In establishing a righteous community, the Teacher advocates for discipline and correction as vital components of ethical living. His writings emphasize that righteous living requires accountability and that failure to address misconduct within the community can lead to spiritual decay. This perspective mirrors the scriptural instruction in Proverbs 12:1, "Whoever loves discipline loves knowledge, but he who hates reproof is stupid."

The Teacher's approach to discipline is not punitive but corrective, aiming to restore members who have strayed from the path of righteousness. By enforcing accountability, the Teacher seeks to uphold the community's standard of holiness and ensure that each member remains committed to God's commandments. This practice reflects a proactive stance in safeguarding the community's ethical integrity, affirming that the pursuit of righteousness requires vigilance and mutual support among the members.

Loving-Kindness and Compassion

Despite his rigorous ethical standards, the Teacher does not neglect the virtues of compassion and loving-kindness. His teachings reveal a balance between strict adherence to God's commandments and the exercise of mercy, especially towards those who demonstrate repentance. This balance is echoed in passages such as Zechariah 7:9, "Thus says Jehovah of hosts, 'Render true judgments, show kindness and mercy to one another.'"

The Teacher's inclusion of compassion within his ethical framework demonstrates his understanding that righteousness is incomplete without love for others. This teaching aligns with the broader biblical mandate to love one's neighbor, illustrating that ethical living in the Qumran community involves both justice and mercy. The Teacher's call for compassion serves as a reminder that the community's mission of righteousness includes bearing one another's burdens and supporting those in need of spiritual guidance.

Faithfulness and Endurance in the Face of Adversity

The Teacher of Righteousness often highlights the need for endurance, especially given the community's isolated position and the opposition they face from external forces. This call for steadfastness in righteousness resonates with passages such as James 1:12, which states, "Blessed is the man who remains steadfast under trial, for when he has stood the test he will receive the crown of life."

The Teacher's encouragement to endure reflects his understanding that ethical living is not always met with immediate reward; instead, it requires a long-term commitment to God's promises. His writings suggest that endurance itself is an expression of righteousness, demonstrating unwavering faith even in the face of persecution or hardship. By promoting endurance, the Teacher prepares the community to stand firm in their ethical commitments, upholding the values of righteousness until the fulfillment of God's purposes.

Conclusion: The Lasting Influence of the Teacher's Ethical Teachings

The ethical teachings of the Teacher of Righteousness provide a comprehensive view of righteousness that integrates separation from sin, obedience to God, justice, humility, discipline, compassion, and endurance. Through his instructions, the Teacher established a standard for living that reflects an unwavering dedication to Jehovah's commandments. These teachings continue to resonate as a model of ethical living rooted in the belief that righteousness encompasses both a commitment to holiness and an active expression of love and mercy within the community.

CHAPTER 19 Unresolved Mysteries: What We Still Don't Know

Introduction: The Enduring Enigma of the Teacher of Righteousness

The Teacher of Righteousness, as portrayed in the Dead Sea Scrolls, remains a compelling yet enigmatic figure. Despite the depth of knowledge the scrolls provide, there are gaps and ambiguities in the historical record that have led to ongoing questions regarding his true identity, his life, and the broader context in which he lived. Scholars have grappled with these uncertainties, examining the Teacher's life, influence, and legacy through the remaining documents, yet several core mysteries endure. These unresolved aspects create an aura of mystery around the Teacher, leaving significant questions about the precise nature of his role, his interactions with historical figures of his time, and the full extent of his teachings.

The scrolls reference him in ways that are often cryptic and allusive, leaving room for interpretation, debate, and intrigue. Some fragments describe him as a righteous leader and prophet, while others indicate that he may have been persecuted by the figure known as the Wicked Priest. Despite these tantalizing glimpses, the absence of explicit detail makes it challenging to draw definitive conclusions. Through examining these lingering questions, we can better appreciate the complexity of the Teacher's legacy and the impact of his teachings on the Qumran community and subsequent scholarship.

The Teacher's True Identity: Who Was He?

One of the most persistent questions surrounding the Teacher of Righteousness is his actual identity. While he is frequently mentioned as a pivotal figure within the Qumran community, the Dead Sea Scrolls do not provide clear biographical information. This gap has led to speculation and varying theories, each of which attempts to piece together the Teacher's background, social position, and potential links to known historical figures. Some scholars have proposed that the Teacher was a high-ranking Jewish priest who came into conflict with the Jerusalem priesthood, possibly around the second century B.C.E. Such a theory aligns with references in the scrolls to the Teacher's authority over matters of law and interpretation, suggesting that he held a respected position among his followers.

Another proposal suggests that the Teacher of Righteousness may have been a zealous leader of a reformist faction, challenging the corruption he perceived within the established religious authorities. This would explain his rivalry with the Wicked Priest and the calls within the scrolls for purity and separation. However, no historical sources outside the Dead Sea Scrolls directly reference an individual who fits all the characteristics attributed to the Teacher, leaving the question of his identity unresolved. This gap underscores the mystery of the Teacher's origin, compelling scholars to rely on circumstantial evidence and interpretive insights from the scrolls themselves.

The Historical Context: When Did the Teacher of Righteousness Live?

The scrolls provide limited chronological markers, making it difficult to place the Teacher within a specific historical period. Many scholars suggest that he likely lived sometime between the second and first centuries B.C.E., a time of significant turmoil and reform within Judaism. This period saw the rise of the Maccabean revolt, conflicts over the high priesthood, and ideological divisions among Jewish factions. Some argue that the Teacher's criticism of the Wicked Priest aligns with the political and religious tensions of this era, especially regarding disputes over the priesthood and temple practices.

However, without precise dates or corroborative historical accounts, it is challenging to pinpoint the Teacher's activities within this turbulent timeframe. This lack of specificity means that even fundamental questions—such as whether the Teacher was a contemporary of the Maccabees or a later figure during the Hasmonean dynasty—remain unresolved. Given the scrolls' frequent use of symbolic language and indirect references, establishing a clear timeline continues to be a formidable challenge for scholars.

The Nature of the Teacher's Conflict with the Wicked Priest

One of the most intriguing aspects of the Teacher's life is his conflict with the figure identified as the Wicked Priest. This adversarial relationship is mentioned in several scrolls, suggesting that it was a defining feature of the Teacher's experience and mission. The Wicked Priest is often depicted as a corrupt authority, possibly a high priest who opposed the Teacher's teachings and sought to undermine his influence within the community. The nature of this opposition, however, remains ambiguous. Was the Wicked Priest a political rival, a religious adversary, or both?

Some scholars posit that the Wicked Priest was part of the established religious order in Jerusalem, representing a faction that opposed the Teacher's reforms. This would imply that the conflict was not merely personal but rooted in fundamental disagreements over religious interpretation, purity laws, and community leadership. Alternatively, it is possible that the Wicked Priest and the Teacher clashed over broader issues, such as the legitimacy of certain temple practices or political alliances with Hellenistic rulers. Despite the scrolls' descriptions, the identity and motivations of the Wicked Priest remain shrouded in mystery, and the precise details of his rivalry with the Teacher elude definitive understanding.

The Scope of the Teacher's Influence: How Far Did His Teachings Spread?

While it is evident that the Teacher of Righteousness held significant sway over the Qumran community, questions remain regarding the full extent of his influence. Did his teachings impact only a small, isolated group, or did they reach broader audiences within the Jewish population of his time? The scrolls suggest that his followers viewed him as a prophet and a divinely inspired leader, yet there is little evidence that his influence extended beyond the Qumran community. This raises questions about whether the Teacher's message was intended for a limited audience or if external factors, such as opposition from the established priesthood, prevented his teachings from gaining wider acceptance.

The absence of references to the Teacher of Righteousness in contemporary historical sources adds to this ambiguity. If the

Teacher's ideas were confined to a relatively small group, it would align with the separatist stance often attributed to the Qumran community. However, it is also conceivable that his teachings may have indirectly influenced other Jewish sects, especially those concerned with purity, scriptural interpretation, and resistance to Hellenistic influences. The lack of clarity regarding the Teacher's broader impact highlights the enduring mystery of his legacy and the scope of his intended audience.

The Teacher's Prophetic Role: Was He Viewed as a Messiah?

Another unresolved question concerns the Teacher's perceived role within his community. Some references in the scrolls imply that he was viewed as a prophet or a divinely inspired leader, yet there is little evidence to suggest that he claimed or was attributed the title of "Messiah." Unlike later messianic figures within Judaism who anticipated a dramatic intervention to restore Israel's sovereignty, the Teacher's mission appears to have focused on spiritual and ethical renewal. Nevertheless, his followers may have regarded him as a unique vessel for God's revelations, fulfilling a special role as a teacher and interpreter of divine wisdom.

This lack of messianic attribution is particularly noteworthy given the eschatological themes present in the Dead Sea Scrolls. The absence of any explicit messianic claims suggests that the Teacher's role was distinct from that of traditional messianic figures. Yet, it remains unclear whether the Qumran community believed the Teacher would be succeeded by a future messiah or if his role was seen as a fulfillment of eschatological expectations. This ambiguity reflects the complexity of the Teacher's spiritual mission, emphasizing his position as a reformer rather than a redeemer.

The End of the Teacher's Life: What Happened to Him?

The Dead Sea Scrolls are notably silent on the fate of the Teacher of Righteousness. This lack of information has led to various theories regarding the end of his life, with some suggesting that he may have died as a result of persecution by the Wicked Priest or other adversaries. Other scholars speculate that he may have continued his work within the community until a natural death, after which his followers preserved and expanded upon his teachings. The scrolls' silence on this matter creates an atmosphere of unresolved tension, hinting at the possibility of martyrdom but leaving the details ambiguous.

If the Teacher's death was indeed a result of persecution, it would underscore the intensity of his conflict with the established religious authorities. Alternatively, if he passed away peacefully within the community, this would suggest that his teachings were ultimately preserved without overt threat from external forces. The uncertainty surrounding the end of his life contributes to the enigmatic nature of his legacy, leaving his followers—and later generations—with an incomplete narrative of his mission.

Conclusion: The Lasting Impact of the Teacher's Mysteries

The unanswered questions surrounding the Teacher of Righteousness underscore the complexity of his role within the Qumran community and the challenges associated with interpreting the Dead Sea Scrolls. These mysteries, ranging from his identity to the nature of his teachings and his relationship with the Wicked Priest, continue to captivate scholars and readers alike. While the scrolls provide valuable insights into his ethics, worldview, and leadership, they stop short of offering a comprehensive account of his life and influence. The enduring mystery of the Teacher of Righteousness invites ongoing exploration, ensuring that his legacy remains a subject of fascination and scholarly inquiry.

Edward D. Andrews

CHAPTER 20 The Enduring Impact of the Teacher of Righteousness

Introduction: The Teacher's Lasting Influence on Faith and Doctrine

The Teacher of Righteousness, central to the thought and practices of the Qumran community, left a significant legacy that continues to captivate scholars and students of the Dead Sea Scrolls. His teachings, example, and uncompromising dedication to purity and scriptural obedience shaped the spiritual and ethical framework of the community, influencing their interpretation of the Law and their expectations of divine judgment. While the details of the Teacher's life and identity remain somewhat enigmatic, the enduring impact of his presence is evident in the scrolls and in the ongoing interest his life has sparked in the study of Second Temple Judaism.

The Teacher's influence extended beyond his immediate community, shaping later interpretations of apocalyptic prophecy, religious purity, and the role of a devout leader under divine guidance. This chapter will examine how the Teacher's impact endured within the Qumran community, how his vision of righteousness and separation influenced their practices, and how the concepts he espoused continued to resonate long after his time, ultimately contributing to broader theological and spiritual discussions within Judaism and providing a framework for early Christian and subsequent scholarly understandings.

The Teacher's Ethical Teachings: A Standard of Righteousness

The Teacher's guidance on righteousness became the moral and ethical bedrock of the Qumran community. His teachings urged an uncompromising adherence to God's commandments as interpreted through a rigorous understanding of the Torah. This emphasis on righteousness, seen as a strict obedience to divine law, encouraged a lifestyle marked by separation from the perceived corrupt influences of the outside world. The Teacher's ethical vision, as encapsulated in the scrolls, is rooted in a distinct understanding of purity and holiness.

This emphasis on righteousness can be connected to biblical passages that call for separation from unholy practices and dedication to God's standards, such as Leviticus 11:44, which says, "For I am Jehovah your God; consecrate yourselves therefore, and be holy, for I am holy." This verse embodies the principle of holiness the Teacher instilled in his followers, urging them to live a life distinctly set apart from the world's defilement. Such separation required vigilance in daily conduct, ritual practices, and even thought life, as they aspired to emulate the Teacher's example of moral purity.

The Qumran community's view of righteousness extended into legal and judicial matters. The Teacher of Righteousness provided interpretations of the law that became the community's guide, indicating that righteousness extended beyond mere ritual but also encompassed social interactions and community structure. This holistic approach to righteousness as an all-encompassing standard helped establish a cohesive identity for the community, one focused on achieving spiritual integrity.

Scriptural Interpretation: The Teacher's Lasting Hermeneutical Approach

One of the most significant impacts of the Teacher of Righteousness was his approach to scriptural interpretation, particularly his focus on prophetic and apocalyptic texts. This interpretive framework, sometimes known as pesher interpretation, involved seeing the scriptures as containing hidden, divine meanings that would only be fully revealed to a divinely inspired leader. By reinterpreting ancient prophecies to apply to the contemporary context of the Qumran community, the Teacher provided his followers with a framework for understanding the unfolding of divine history.

This approach to interpretation can be linked to passages such as Daniel 12:9, where Jehovah says, "Go your way, Daniel, for the words are shut up and sealed until the time of the end." Here, the concept of sealed revelation aligns with the Teacher's understanding that God's plans would be revealed progressively to the righteous. The Teacher's interpretations, often specific to his time and setting, provided the community with a unique lens through which to view current events, understand their trials, and anticipate future vindication from God.

Through this interpretive lens, the Teacher offered explanations of scriptural prophecies that centered on the community's experiences and struggles. His role as the revealer of divine secrets solidified his authority and provided a sense of divine purpose and destiny. The scrolls reflect this approach through the numerous interpretations and applications of prophetic passages that reinforce the community's distinct role in God's plan, helping to shape an eschatological worldview that defined their daily lives and spiritual aspirations.

An Apocalyptic Vision of Justice and Vindication

The Teacher of Righteousness profoundly influenced the Qumran community's eschatological outlook, which centered on themes of divine judgment, the coming of a final redemption, and the vindication of the righteous. The Teacher instilled an unwavering belief in a coming judgment that would purify Israel, exposing and punishing the wicked while rewarding those who had upheld the covenant. This vision of divine justice, often described in apocalyptic terms, was intended to motivate the community to endure hardship and maintain their faithfulness, knowing that their suffering had an ultimate purpose.

This apocalyptic worldview aligns with the sentiments expressed in passages such as Isaiah 26:21: "For behold, Jehovah is coming out of his place to punish the inhabitants of the earth for their iniquity, and the earth will disclose the blood shed on it, and will no more cover its slain." Such verses echo the Teacher's emphasis on divine retribution and vindication for the righteous, resonating with his calls for unwavering obedience in the face of persecution and opposition. The community's belief in this coming judgment underscored their separation from mainstream Judaism, reinforcing their identity as the true "sons of light" who would stand righteous before God on the day of reckoning.

The expectation of imminent judgment and the promise of God's justice gave the community a profound sense of purpose. This vision not only provided comfort amidst suffering but also shaped the ethical and ritualistic boundaries that defined them. By establishing such boundaries, the Teacher reinforced the community's commitment to purity and loyalty to Jehovah, distinguishing them as a remnant preserved for divine vindication.

The Teacher's Influence on Qumran's Rituals and Communal Life

The Teacher of Righteousness left an indelible mark on the Qumran community's practices, particularly in terms of ritual purity and communal organization. His teachings emphasized strict adherence to purity laws, viewing ritual purity as a tangible expression of spiritual devotion. This adherence extended to every facet of life, including dietary restrictions, purification rites, and Sabbath observance. By elevating these practices, the Teacher underscored the need for holiness in preparation for the coming judgment.

This concept of ritual purity aligns with Leviticus 20:26, which says, "You shall be holy to me, for I, Jehovah, am holy and have separated you from the peoples, that you should be mine." This verse reflects the theological foundation for the community's emphasis on maintaining purity and separation from defiling influences. The Teacher's instructions led to the development of strict rules that governed the community's lifestyle, fostering a disciplined environment where every member was committed to upholding the covenant.

Moreover, the Teacher's teachings influenced the organizational structure of the Qumran community. The scrolls outline hierarchical roles and responsibilities, with the Teacher of Righteousness depicted as a spiritual guide and arbiter of divine law. His position as both a religious authority and a practical leader set a precedent for communal governance, establishing an order that reflected both obedience to divine mandates and mutual accountability. Through this structure, the Teacher's influence shaped a distinctively cohesive community, one that saw itself as uniquely devoted to fulfilling God's purpose.

Influence on Later Religious Thought: A Legacy Beyond Qumran

While the immediate impact of the Teacher of Righteousness was most evident within the Qumran community, his teachings have had a lasting influence on broader religious thought. The Teacher's focus on ethical purity, his distinctive interpretation of prophetic texts, and his apocalyptic vision contributed to the larger spiritual landscape of Second Temple Judaism. Elements of the Teacher's legacy can be observed in the rise of later Jewish sects that emphasized rigorous adherence to the Law and an anticipation of divine judgment.

The Teacher's legacy also extends into the study of early Christian thought, where comparisons have often been drawn between the Qumran community's focus on eschatology and the New Testament's themes of divine judgment, purity, and community. While the Teacher was not directly connected to Christian doctrine, his influence provides valuable context for understanding the diverse religious environment in which early Christianity emerged. The shared themes of covenant loyalty, the anticipation of God's kingdom, and the need for righteous endurance all reflect an enduring spiritual heritage shaped by the Teacher's teachings.

The Teacher of Righteousness remains a figure whose teachings and example offer insight into the religious fervor and theological priorities of his time. His impact, preserved in the Dead Sea Scrolls, continues to inform modern scholarship and deepen our understanding of ancient religious movements that shaped the beliefs and practices of subsequent generations.

SECTION 2 The Wicked Priest: The Adversary of the Teacher of Righteousness

Edward D. Andrews

CHAPTER 21 The Wicked Priest in the Dead Sea Scrolls

The Identity of the Wicked Priest: Historical and Contextual Considerations

The "Wicked Priest" emerges as a significant antagonist within the Dead Sea Scrolls, representing the opposing forces faced by the Teacher of Righteousness. The Dead Sea Scrolls, primarily authored by members of the Qumran community, depict a theological and moral struggle between righteousness and corruption, with the Wicked Priest embodying the community's view of corrupt leadership. This figure is portrayed as a Jewish leader who violated the covenant, leading the people astray and opposing the teachings and moral integrity of the Teacher of Righteousness.

The identity of the Wicked Priest has been a subject of debate among scholars, as the Dead Sea Scrolls do not explicitly name him but offer clues based on his actions, titles, and his association with specific historical events. Certain scrolls, including the *Habakkuk Commentary* (1QpHab), provide descriptions of the Wicked Priest's conduct, his character, and his antagonistic actions against the Teacher. By examining the Wicked Priest's attributes and activities, it becomes clear that he is more than a mere individual; he represents a broader spiritual conflict.

The Wicked Priest's identity is often associated with certain high priests from the Second Temple period, specifically during the Hasmonean dynasty. Some suggest he may have been one of the high priests from the era of late 2nd century to early 1st century B.C.E., typically around **150–76 B.C.E.**, a time marked by political strife and religious corruption. The characteristics attributed to the Wicked Priest align with accusations of impurity, hypocrisy, and material greed, distinguishing him as a figure condemned for his lack of adherence to the covenantal values that the Teacher of Righteousness upheld.

Moral and Spiritual Corruption: The Wicked Priest's Actions Against the Teacher

The moral and spiritual corruption of the Wicked Priest is vividly portrayed in the Dead Sea Scrolls. His actions are depicted as diametrically opposed to the righteousness embodied by the Teacher. The Wicked Priest is accused of violating sacred temple practices, defiling the sanctuary, and using his position to benefit himself at the expense of his spiritual responsibilities. This behavior represents a complete disregard for the covenant that binds the people of Israel to God's standards, contrasting sharply with the reverence for holiness and purity upheld by the Teacher of Righteousness.

In the *Habakkuk Commentary*, the Wicked Priest is described as one who "trusted in his riches" and "rebelled against God." This depiction aligns with warnings in the Scriptures against materialism and self-centeredness, such as in Proverbs 28:20: "A faithful man will abound with blessings, but whoever hastens to be rich will not go unpunished." This verse captures the essence of the Wicked Priest's failure, as he placed his trust in wealth and personal ambition rather than in his duty to serve God and uphold the covenant.

This moral failure of the Wicked Priest is further underscored in his treatment of the Teacher of Righteousness. The Wicked Priest is portrayed as actively seeking to harm the Teacher, engaging in actions that go beyond mere opposition to physical confrontation and persecution. These antagonistic actions illustrate the broader conflict between righteousness and unrighteousness, with the Teacher standing as a symbol of faithfulness to God's covenant and the Wicked Priest embodying a betrayal of that sacred relationship.

Theological Implications of the Wicked Priest's Opposition to the Teacher

The struggle between the Teacher of Righteousness and the Wicked Priest is not merely a personal conflict; it carries profound theological implications. In opposing the Teacher, the Wicked Priest challenges the very foundations of divine justice and covenantal faithfulness. His actions signify a resistance to God's purposes and a rejection of the spiritual standards that the Qumran community held dear. The Wicked Priest's antagonism can be seen as a manifestation of the broader battle between good and evil, a theme prevalent throughout the Scriptures.

The description of the Wicked Priest as one who profanes the sanctuary and disregards the law parallels Old Testament accounts of leaders who fell from God's favor due to disobedience. For instance, in 1 Samuel 15:23, it is stated, "For rebellion is as the sin of divination, and presumption is as iniquity and idolatry." This verse encapsulates the essence of the Wicked Priest's rebellion, which reflects not only a defiance against the Teacher of Righteousness but a broader defiance against God's established order.

In this light, the Wicked Priest's role in the Dead Sea Scrolls serves as a cautionary example of what happens when a leader departs from God's ways. His opposition to the Teacher represents a theological conflict where the struggle for purity, truth, and obedience to God's covenant stands in stark contrast to the self-serving and corrupt actions of a compromised leader. The Qumran community saw in the Wicked Priest a figure whose failures validated their separation from mainstream Judaism and affirmed their pursuit of a more authentic, uncorrupted faith.

Divine Judgment and the Fate of the Wicked Priest

The Dead Sea Scrolls vividly depict the Qumran community's belief in an inevitable divine judgment that would befall the Wicked Priest due to his moral corruption and opposition to the Teacher of Righteousness. This expectation of judgment reinforces the community's theology that God holds all individuals accountable, especially leaders, for maintaining the integrity of His covenant. The Qumran community saw the Wicked Priest as emblematic of corrupt leadership within mainstream Judaism and anticipated that Jehovah would bring this figure to account for his betrayal and sins.

According to the *Habakkuk Commentary* (1QpHab), divine retribution is portrayed as certain and severe. The Wicked Priest is depicted as "pursuing" the Teacher on a day "appointed for atonement" and attempting to bring harm upon him. However, this assault on a holy figure is perceived as a direct affront to Jehovah, aligning with Psalm 105:15: "Do not touch my anointed ones, do my prophets no harm." The community believed that such acts of opposition against the Teacher would ultimately invoke God's wrath, demonstrating that no defilement of sacred duties would go unnoticed by the Almighty.

The fate of the Wicked Priest aligns with broader Old Testament warnings against corrupt leaders. For instance, Ezekiel 34 denounces the "shepherds of Israel" who exploited their position for selfish gain, forsaking the well-being of the people. Ezekiel 34:10 warns, "Thus says Jehovah God, Behold, I am against the shepherds, and I will require my sheep at their hand and put a stop to their feeding the sheep." This indictment parallels the Qumran community's view of the Wicked Priest as a derelict leader whose time of reckoning would inevitably arrive through divine intervention.

The Significance of the Wicked Priest as an Archetype of Apostasy

Beyond a historical figure, the Wicked Priest also represents a broader archetype of spiritual apostasy. His actions illustrate a profound departure from the values held by the Teacher and the Qumran community, demonstrating how one entrusted with sacred duties can fall into moral compromise. This concept of apostasy is a recurring theme throughout the Bible, where individuals or groups abandon covenantal faithfulness for personal gain or to appease worldly influences.

In Deuteronomy 13:5, the law warns Israel against such apostasy: "But that prophet or that dreamer of dreams shall be put to death, because he has taught rebellion against Jehovah your God." This passage underscores the severity with which God views those who mislead His people, portraying apostasy as a crime that leads to judgment. The Wicked Priest embodies this warning, serving as an example of how even those in positions of religious authority are not exempt from divine accountability.

The Qumran community saw in the Wicked Priest a reason for their own separation from mainstream Jewish practices. They viewed themselves as the "remnant," faithful to Jehovah's commands in a way that had been forsaken by the priesthood represented by the Wicked Priest. This perspective parallels the idea of a faithful remnant in the Scriptures, as seen in passages like Isaiah 1:9: "If Jehovah of hosts had not left us a few survivors, we would have been like Sodom, and we would have been like Gomorrah." The community believed that their faithfulness stood in contrast to the Wicked Priest's apostasy, affirming their role as bearers of true covenantal integrity.

Lessons on Righteous Leadership: The Contrast Between the Teacher and the Wicked Priest

The Dead Sea Scrolls underscore the necessity of righteous leadership by presenting the stark contrast between the Teacher of Righteousness and the Wicked Priest. This dichotomy reflects a broader Biblical principle that leaders are called to a higher standard of accountability. The Scriptures highlight numerous examples where leaders are either exalted or condemned based on their adherence to God's commands.

In Proverbs 29:2, it is stated, "When the righteous increase, the people rejoice, but when the wicked rule, the people groan." This sentiment resonates with the Qumran community's discontent with the religious leadership of their time. They saw the Wicked Priest as a cause of spiritual corruption, while the Teacher of Righteousness symbolized the qualities they believed were essential for a godly leader: humility, adherence to the law, and devotion to Jehovah's will.

The community's emphasis on righteousness and separation from corrupt influences mirrors the Biblical call for holiness, as seen in Leviticus 11:44: "For I am Jehovah your God. Consecrate yourselves therefore, and be holy, for I am holy." The Wicked Priest's failure to uphold this standard solidified the Qumran community's conviction to remain apart, affirming their identity as a pure assembly in contrast to the compromised leadership represented by the Wicked Priest.

Conclusion of Judgment and Vindication

In the Qumran texts, the expectation of judgment on the Wicked Priest is accompanied by a promise of vindication for the Teacher of Righteousness and his followers. This prophetic vindication reflects the ultimate justice anticipated by the community, where the faithful would be rewarded and the unrighteous punished. Their belief that Jehovah would intervene to rectify the wrongs committed by the Wicked Priest reassured them of God's sovereignty and affirmed their commitment to their unique interpretation of the law and the covenant.

The eschatological nature of the community's beliefs also highlighted their expectation that Jehovah's justice would not only address present injustices but also establish an eternal reign of righteousness. The concept of divine vindication for the righteous is deeply rooted in Scripture, as seen in passages like Isaiah 35:4: "Say to those who have an anxious heart, 'Be strong; fear not! Behold, your God will come with vengeance, with the recompense of God. He will come and save you.'" This expectation of deliverance reinforced the Qumran community's faith in Jehovah's ultimate judgment and their hope for future redemption from all forms of oppression and unrighteousness.

In conclusion, the Wicked Priest stands as a pivotal figure within the Dead Sea Scrolls, embodying a complex blend of historical opposition, theological conflict, and moral corruption. His role as the adversary of the Teacher of Righteousness reveals much about the Qumran community's values, their commitment to covenantal faithfulness, and their belief in Jehovah's ultimate justice. Through the contrast between the Wicked Priest and the Teacher of Righteousness, the scrolls underscore a profound truth: God's expectations of holiness and integrity remain steadfast, and any deviation from these standards is met with accountability, as demonstrated in the anticipated judgment upon the Wicked Priest.

CHAPTER 22 The Identity of the Wicked Priest: Historical Theories

What Historical Theories Surround the Identity of the Wicked Priest?

The figure of the Wicked Priest in the Dead Sea Scrolls has intrigued scholars and believers alike, providing insight into the complex relationships, theological disagreements, and moral conflicts that shaped the religious communities of ancient Israel. Historically, the Wicked Priest is presented as a significant opponent to the Teacher of Righteousness, embodying characteristics of corruption, apostasy, and ultimately divine judgment. The Dead Sea Scrolls, particularly the *Habakkuk Commentary* (1QpHab), give glimpses into this enigmatic figure, though they do not reveal his name explicitly. Over the centuries, various historical theories have emerged regarding his identity, largely informed by the socio-political climate of ancient Judaism and the distinct roles of the priesthood and ruling authorities. This chapter explores prominent theories surrounding the Wicked Priest, his actions, and his historical setting.

How Do the Dead Sea Scrolls Describe the Wicked Priest?

The Dead Sea Scrolls refer to the Wicked Priest using terms that highlight his moral failings and betrayal of sacred responsibilities. He is characterized as someone who "chased after" the Teacher of Righteousness with the intent of harming him. In the *Habakkuk Commentary*, the Wicked Priest is depicted as one who sought personal gain at the expense of his spiritual integrity, with statements suggesting that he "ruled over Israel" but did so with unrighteous intentions, abandoning the faithful observance of the covenant. This portrayal not only defines his role in direct opposition to the Teacher but also underscores the Qumran community's disdain for leadership that fell short of the standards they believed were mandated by Jehovah.

The description of the Wicked Priest aligns with broader themes found in Scripture, where leaders who fail to uphold the covenant and lead righteously face condemnation. Malachi 2:7-8, for instance, rebukes the priests of Israel for failing in their duty: "For the lips of a priest should guard knowledge, and people should seek instruction from his mouth, for he is the messenger of Jehovah of hosts. But you have turned aside from the way. You have caused many to stumble by your instruction." This kind of apostasy among the priests would resonate deeply with the Qumran community, who saw themselves as a separated group committed to faithfulness amidst widespread corruption.

Which Historical Figures Have Been Proposed as the Wicked Priest?

Several historical figures have been suggested as the Wicked Priest, each theory based on specific characteristics, dates, and events described within the Dead Sea Scrolls. These theories focus on the idea that the Wicked Priest was not merely a symbolic figure but rather a specific person in Jewish history. The theories typically center around prominent leaders in the Hasmonean dynasty, given their role in the priesthood and the heightened tensions of the Second Temple period.

Jonathan Apphus (High Priest, 152–143 B.C.E.)

One of the earliest proposed candidates for the Wicked Priest is Jonathan Apphus, a prominent member of the Hasmonean dynasty. As a leader who rose to power amidst political turmoil, Jonathan held both priestly and political authority, consolidating power in a way that was viewed as controversial. Although the Hasmonean family initially championed a return to Jewish sovereignty and the purity of the faith, they eventually adopted Hellenistic customs and power structures, which may have led to their estrangement from more conservative Jewish factions.

The Qumran community may have seen Jonathan as the Wicked Priest due to his departure from what they considered to be the priestly norms established by Jehovah. His involvement in political maneuvering and alliances with foreign powers could have been viewed as a direct betrayal of covenantal values. The suspicion is that Jonathan's pursuit of political power compromised his faithfulness to the covenant, echoing the traits attributed to the Wicked Priest.

Simon Thassi (High Priest, 143–135 B.C.E.)

Another candidate often suggested as the Wicked Priest is Simon Thassi, the brother of Jonathan and his successor in the high priesthood. Simon consolidated his authority, securing recognition from the Seleucid Empire and even receiving the title of "ethnarch." Although his rule brought stability and prosperity, Simon's alignment with foreign rulers may have been seen as a betrayal by groups that desired absolute independence and pure worship practices, untouched by political compromises.

The Qumran community, with its strict adherence to covenantal purity and separation from external influences, could have viewed Simon's acceptance of titles and recognition from secular authorities as an act of spiritual compromise, fitting the character of the Wicked Priest. This view resonates with passages like Isaiah 52:11, "Depart, depart, go out from there! Touch no unclean thing; go out from the midst of her; purify yourselves, you who bear the vessels of Jehovah," underscoring the community's call to purity and separation from worldly powers.

John Hyrcanus I (High Priest, 135–104 B.C.E.)

John Hyrcanus I is frequently proposed as the Wicked Priest due to his lengthy reign and his active role in both religious and military leadership. As a high priest who also expanded Jewish territory through military campaigns, Hyrcanus wielded considerable influence. His rule, however, involved alliances with Hellenistic powers and policies that diverged from traditional covenantal values, such as the forced conversion of Idumeans to Judaism.

For the Qumran community, these actions might have epitomized the abandonment of covenantal purity. The community's disdain for forced conversions and religious compromises would align well with the portrayal of Hyrcanus as the Wicked Priest. Jeremiah 3:6-7 reflects Jehovah's reproach of apostate leaders: "During the days of King Josiah, Jehovah said to me, 'Have you seen what faithless Israel has done? She has gone up on every high hill and under every green tree, and there has played the whore. And I thought, After she has done all this, she will return to me, but she did not return.'"

Alexander Jannaeus (High Priest, 103–76 B.C.E.)

Alexander Jannaeus, known for his turbulent rule and conflicts with various Jewish factions, is perhaps the most widely proposed figure as the Wicked Priest. Jannaeus engaged in multiple conflicts with Pharisees and other groups that opposed his authoritarian rule, even reportedly ordering the massacre of dissenters. His reign was characterized by open hostility toward the Pharisees and an often violent suppression of those who questioned his authority.

The *Habakkuk Commentary*'s depiction of the Wicked Priest pursuing the Teacher of Righteousness and seeking his harm aligns closely with Jannaeus' reputation for violent opposition to those who opposed him. The actions of Jannaeus would have exemplified the traits of a leader who abandoned covenantal responsibility in pursuit of power, fitting the portrayal of the Wicked Priest. Proverbs 29:12 warns against corrupt leadership, stating, "If a ruler listens to falsehood, all his officials will be wicked," reflecting the Qumran community's perception of the pervasive corruption under Jannaeus' rule.

Why Did the Qumran Community See the Wicked Priest as a Threat?

The Qumran community's perception of the Wicked Priest as a threat extended beyond individual actions; it was rooted in a theological concern for the preservation of covenantal purity and adherence to divine law. They believed that the priesthood held a sacred role that required strict adherence to the covenant, untainted by political ambitions or alliances with foreign powers. The Wicked Priest, regardless of his specific identity, represented a departure from these principles and posed a risk to the sanctity of Israel's relationship with Jehovah.

In the Qumran community's eyes, the Wicked Priest threatened the core values of their faith. His political alliances, departure from covenantal teachings, and possible violence toward the Teacher of Righteousness undermined the very foundation of their belief in a faithful remnant chosen by Jehovah. This sentiment is echoed in 1 Samuel 2:30, where Jehovah declares, "For those who honor me I will honor, and those who despise me shall be lightly esteemed." The community saw themselves as upholding this principle, in contrast to the Wicked Priest's perceived dishonor of God's covenant.

How Did the Wicked Priest Influence the Qumran Community's Separation?

The character of the Wicked Priest played a significant role in shaping the Qumran community's decision to separate from mainstream Judaism. They believed that the religious authorities in Jerusalem, represented by the Wicked Priest, had compromised their sacred responsibilities and thus could no longer be trusted to lead the people in righteousness. This conviction led the community to establish an alternative society, dedicated to covenantal faithfulness and rigorous observance of the law.

Isaiah 52:11 speaks to this separation, calling on believers to depart from corruption: "Depart, depart, go out from there! Touch no unclean thing; go out from the midst of her; purify yourselves, you who bear the vessels of Jehovah." The Qumran community saw themselves as heeding this call, setting themselves apart from a priesthood that they believed had become defiled. The Wicked Priest thus became a catalyst for their distinct identity, shaping their practices, beliefs, and commitment to a pure community.

Conclusion of Divine Judgment Awaiting the Wicked Priest

The Qumran community's writings imply a divine judgment awaiting the Wicked Priest, emphasizing Jehovah's ultimate authority over those in leadership. They believed that the actions of the Wicked Priest would not go unpunished, trusting that Jehovah would enact justice on behalf of His covenant. This expectation is echoed in Isaiah 5:20: "Woe to those who call evil good and good evil," capturing the community's anticipation of a time when corrupt leadership would be held accountable.

In summary, the identity of the Wicked Priest remains a subject of historical analysis, with theories surrounding Jonathan Apphus, Simon Thassi, John Hyrcanus, and Alexander Jannaeus offering different perspectives on this enigmatic figure. Each potential candidate reflects traits condemned by the Qumran community, who viewed the Wicked Priest as a symbol of the dangers posed by political and spiritual compromise. Through their understanding of this figure, the Qumran community sought to uphold the sanctity of the covenant and the teachings of Jehovah, ultimately reinforcing their commitment to a life of separation and righteousness.

CHAPTER 23 Theological Differences Between the Teacher and the Wicked Priest

The Context of Theological Conflict in the Qumran Community

The theological tension between the Teacher of Righteousness and the Wicked Priest, as evidenced in the Dead Sea Scrolls, highlights two distinct and opposing approaches to worship, obedience, and the interpretation of the covenantal relationship with Jehovah. This enmity is not merely personal but underscores a deeper, ideological struggle over covenant fidelity and righteousness, with each figure embodying a divergent pathway within the Jewish faith. The Dead Sea Scrolls reveal this schism, situating the Teacher of Righteousness as a preserver of the covenant and the Wicked Priest as an agent of corruption.

The Role of Covenant in the Theology of the Teacher and the Wicked Priest

The Teacher of Righteousness adhered strictly to the covenant established by Jehovah with Israel, rooted in obedience, holiness, and separation from ungodly influences. His interpretation emphasized purity, self-sacrifice, and a life wholly dedicated to following Jehovah's statutes. The Teacher's life and teaching aligned closely with the values laid out in Leviticus 11:45, which commands, "I am Jehovah who brought you up out of the land of Egypt to be your God; you shall therefore be holy, for I am holy." This dedication to holiness drove the Teacher to reject any form of compromise or accommodation to worldly values or corrupt influences within religious leadership.

In contrast, the Wicked Priest's theology strayed from these covenantal tenets, aligning instead with a more expedient, pragmatic approach to governance and religion. This divergence is most evident in his dealings with temple practices and political alliances, as he adopted a self-centered, corrupt model of priesthood, prioritizing wealth and power over spiritual integrity. Ezekiel 22:26 highlights a similar condemnation, stating, "Her priests have done violence to my law and have profaned my holy things. They have made no distinction between the holy and the common."

Divergent Views on the Law: Interpretative Rigidity vs. Flexibility

A fundamental theological rift between the Teacher of Righteousness and the Wicked Priest lay in their approach to the Mosaic Law. The Teacher maintained a strict adherence to the law, interpreting it with a rigidity that underscored his devotion to Jehovah's standards. He valued precision in observing the smallest commandments, drawing on passages like Deuteronomy 4:2: "You shall not add to the word that I command you, nor take from it, that you may keep the commandments of Jehovah your God that I command you."

Conversely, the Wicked Priest displayed a lenient approach to the law, viewing it through a lens of expediency that allowed for modifications in favor of political and personal gain. This flexibility is characteristic of leaders who prioritize their agendas over strict adherence to divine ordinances, drawing a stark line between himself and the Teacher. The Wicked Priest's theological framework might be compared to the laxity condemned by Isaiah 29:13: "This people draw near with their mouth and honor me with their lips, while their hearts are far from me, and their fear of me is a commandment taught by men."

Eschatological Expectations: Judgment and Reward

The Teacher's theology placed a significant emphasis on eschatological justice, expecting a divine reckoning that would validate the righteous and condemn the wicked. His teachings were deeply infused with the notion of ultimate accountability before Jehovah, as seen in passages like Psalm 1:5-6, which states, "Therefore the wicked will not stand in the judgment, nor sinners in the congregation of the righteous; for Jehovah knows the way of the righteous, but the way of the wicked will perish." The Teacher conveyed that Jehovah's judgment would expose the falsehood of corrupt leaders, separating those who upheld the covenant from those who betrayed it.

On the contrary, the Wicked Priest seems to have downplayed this eschatological accountability, displaying a more secular worldview that minimized divine judgment in favor of immediate rewards and gains. This approach to theology reflects a materialistic mindset, one that relegates divine judgment to a theoretical status while prioritizing present circumstances. Proverbs 21:30 condemns this short-sighted perspective: "No wisdom, no understanding, no counsel can avail against Jehovah." In this way, the Wicked Priest's disregard for eschatology reflects an unwillingness to recognize the eternal consequences of his actions.

Ritual Purity and Holiness: Sacred vs. Profane

In the theology of the Teacher of Righteousness, purity and holiness were non-negotiable requirements, and they served as the foundation for his community's religious identity. His views aligned with Jehovah's commands in passages like Leviticus 19:2: "You shall be holy, for I Jehovah your God am holy." This belief in purity extended to every aspect of religious life, from personal behavior to communal practices, shaping the strict discipline and lifestyle of the Qumran community.

Conversely, the Wicked Priest showed disregard for the principles of ritual purity, violating the sanctity of his office by engaging in acts that profaned the temple and defiled its sanctity. This sacrilegious behavior is reminiscent of the judgment pronounced in Malachi 1:6-7: "A son honors his father, and a servant his master. If then I am a father, where is my honor? And if I am a master, where is my fear? says Jehovah of hosts to you, O priests, who despise my name." By desecrating the temple with impure actions, the Wicked Priest abandoned the fundamental requirements of his priestly duty, undermining the holiness Jehovah demanded.

Economic Ethics: Material Gain vs. Spiritual Integrity

A clear demarcation in the ethical practices of the Teacher and the Wicked Priest lies in their approach to wealth and material possessions. The Teacher advocated for a life free from greed, embracing the biblical ideal of contentment and trust in Jehovah's provision. This perspective aligns with Proverbs 11:4, which states, "Riches do not profit in the day of wrath, but righteousness delivers from death." For the Teacher, wealth was secondary to spiritual integrity, emphasizing a life of modesty and devotion over material pursuits.

The Wicked Priest, in stark contrast, displayed a blatant pursuit of wealth and luxury, using his religious office to amass riches and indulge in self-serving endeavors. This unethical pursuit of material gain aligns with the condemnation found in Micah 3:11: "Its heads give judgment for a bribe; its priests teach for a price; its prophets practice divination for money; yet they lean on Jehovah and say, 'Is not Jehovah in the midst of us?'" Such behavior underscores the Wicked Priest's deviation from true spiritual service, revealing a heart inclined toward greed rather than righteousness.

Political Alliances: Separation vs. Compromise

The Teacher's theology emphasized a separation from secular influence, as he viewed political alliances as threats to the purity of worship. This stance reflects the biblical principle found in Psalm 146:3, "Put not your trust in princes, in a son of man, in whom there is no salvation." The Teacher encouraged the Qumran community to remain distinct from political powers, warning that such alliances would inevitably lead to spiritual compromise and idolatry.

Conversely, the Wicked Priest sought political alliances, leveraging his position to gain favor and power, even at the cost of religious integrity. His actions echo the warning in Hosea 7:8, where Israel's alliances with foreign nations are condemned: "Ephraim mixes himself with the peoples; Ephraim is a cake not turned." The Wicked Priest's compromise for political security reveals a theology willing to sacrifice divine principles for worldly influence, further demonstrating his divergence from the Teacher's faithful adherence to Jehovah's commands.

Summary of Divergent Theologies: The Righteous vs. the Corrupt

The theological contrasts between the Teacher of Righteousness and the Wicked Priest represent a broader conflict within the Jewish faith during the Second Temple period. These contrasts highlight two opposing paths: one of faithful adherence to Jehovah's covenant and one of self-centered defilement. The Teacher's strict adherence to the Law, his belief in divine judgment, and his commitment to purity and righteousness stand as a testament to a life devoted to Jehovah. Meanwhile, the Wicked Priest's materialism, political entanglements, and disregard for the sanctity of his office reveal a path of corruption and departure from divine commandments.

By examining the theological differences between these two figures, we gain insight into the values and priorities that defined the Qumran community and the motivations behind their separation from mainstream Judaism. This exploration also highlights the enduring relevance of covenantal faithfulness and obedience, serving as a reminder that spiritual integrity remains paramount in the face of worldly compromise and self-interest.

CHAPTER 24 The Wicked Priest and the Corruption of the Temple

The Role of the Wicked Priest in Temple Leadership and Governance

In the Dead Sea Scrolls, the Wicked Priest emerges as a divisive and morally compromised figure. His position as a high priest placed him at the center of religious life in Jerusalem and at the forefront of overseeing temple worship and sacrificial systems. However, unlike the righteous leadership exemplified by the Teacher of Righteousness, the Wicked Priest allowed his role to be dominated by political motivations, personal gain, and secular ambitions. This corruption ran contrary to the biblical expectations for priesthood and temple administration as outlined in Leviticus and Deuteronomy.

The Book of Malachi, which condemns religious leaders who dishonor their roles, aligns closely with the situation of the Wicked Priest: "A son honors his father, and a servant his master. If then I am a father, where is my honor? And if I am a master, where is my fear? says Jehovah of hosts to you, O priests, who despise my name" (Malachi 1:6). This passage mirrors the disrespect the Wicked Priest showed to his position, treating the sacred space as a means to enrich himself rather than honor Jehovah.

Financial Exploitation of Temple Worship

One of the clearest examples of the Wicked Priest's corruption involved his manipulation of temple finances. The temple, which served as both a religious and social hub, received substantial tithes, offerings, and funds dedicated to maintaining religious services. Instead of using these resources for the community's spiritual benefit, the Wicked Priest exploited them for his own financial gain, diverting sacred funds to increase his wealth and power. This exploitation likely fueled the anger and condemnation reflected in the Dead Sea Scrolls, where the Teacher of Righteousness condemns the Wicked Priest's brazen disrespect for the sacred.

Isaiah 56:11 denounces leaders who take advantage of their positions, stating, "The dogs have a mighty appetite; they never have enough. But they are shepherds who have no understanding; they have all turned to their own way, each to his own gain, one and all." Such passages illustrate how the Wicked Priest's greed sharply contrasted with the righteous standard of leadership called for in the Scriptures.

The Compromise of Ritual Purity in Sacrificial Practices

A significant element of temple worship during the Second Temple period involved maintaining rigorous standards of ritual purity, especially in sacrifices offered on behalf of the people. However, the Wicked Priest's actions undermined this sacred responsibility. Historical records and the Dead Sea Scrolls indicate that he allowed and even participated in practices that compromised the purity of sacrifices, which, according to the Law, were intended to be unblemished and offered with reverence (Leviticus 22:20-21).

The Prophet Ezekiel condemns similar abuses, saying, "Her priests have done violence to my law and have profaned my holy things. They have made no distinction between the holy and the common, neither have they taught the difference between the unclean and the clean" (Ezekiel 22:26). Such corruption degraded the sacrifices, dishonoring Jehovah and desecrating the holy rituals that were central to Israel's covenant relationship with Him.

Political Alliances and Compromises

The Wicked Priest's alignment with secular powers served his ambitions but led to a betrayal of the temple's sanctity. By forming alliances with local rulers, he sought to secure his position, consolidate power, and gain political favor, often at the expense of temple integrity and the community's spiritual welfare. Such alliances often required compromises on religious matters, directly contradicting the command for Israel's leaders to remain separate from secular influences (Deuteronomy 7:2-3).

Psalm 146:3 cautions against placing trust in political powers over Jehovah, stating, "Put not your trust in princes, in a son of man, in whom there is no salvation." The Wicked Priest's dependence on political alliances ultimately led to a dilution of religious standards and the abandonment of covenantal principles, forsaking the temple's holy purpose to serve his personal interests.

The Wicked Priest's Failure to Uphold Covenantal Faithfulness

The essence of temple worship was to uphold the covenant between Jehovah and His people, providing a space for atonement, reflection, and communion. The Wicked Priest, however, treated the temple as a means to further his own political and economic agenda rather than maintaining it as a sacred institution devoted to Jehovah. By prioritizing his power and material wealth over covenantal faithfulness, he subverted the very purpose of the temple, turning a place of holiness into a den of corruption.

The denunciation found in Isaiah 1:11-13 reflects Jehovah's disdain for worship devoid of true reverence: "What to me is the multitude of your sacrifices? says Jehovah; I have had enough of burnt offerings of rams and the fat of well-fed beasts; I do not delight in the blood of bulls, or of lambs, or of goats." Jehovah desires genuine worship, and the Wicked Priest's actions epitomized empty ritual without a heart devoted to the covenant.

Abuse of Authority and the Oppression of the Righteous

The Wicked Priest's pursuit of power led him to oppress those who sought to remain faithful to Jehovah, particularly the Teacher of Righteousness and his followers. His persecution of the righteous further highlighted his rejection of the covenant, as he prioritized personal gain over the well-being of the faithful. The Dead Sea Scrolls recount instances of harassment and oppression that the Teacher endured, reflecting the Wicked Priest's disregard for those who adhered to Jehovah's commands.

Proverbs 28:16 warns, "A ruler who lacks understanding is a cruel oppressor, but he who hates unjust gain will prolong his days." The Wicked Priest's oppression of the righteous demonstrates his deviation from Jehovah's commands, embodying the traits of an unjust ruler who values power over righteousness. His actions reveal a profound theological conflict, as he embodied the antithesis of the godly leadership exemplified by the Teacher of Righteousness.

Conclusion: The Profound Impact of the Wicked Priest's Corruption

The theological and ethical failings of the Wicked Priest had far-reaching effects, leading to the desecration of the temple and undermining the community's covenantal relationship with Jehovah. His actions highlight the dangers of self-serving leadership and the consequences of compromising religious principles for personal gain. The Teacher of Righteousness, in contrast, stands as a testament to the enduring value of covenantal faithfulness, embodying the dedication and righteousness that the Wicked Priest so grievously abandoned.

CHAPTER 25 The Political and Religious Power Struggles of the Second Temple Period

The Political Context of the Second Temple Period: The Rise of the Hasmoneans

The Second Temple period, especially the Hasmonean dynasty (142–63 B.C.E.), was marked by intense political shifts and power struggles. Following the Maccabean revolt, the Hasmonean family established a dynasty that merged religious and political authority, creating a hybrid role that deviated from the Davidic model and concentrated power in the hands of high priests. While the Maccabean revolt initially sought religious freedom from Hellenistic oppression, it ultimately led to the Hasmonean high priests' secularization. The Hasmonean leaders ruled with a mix of religious and political authority, abandoning their initial motivations to restore Jehovah's law by incorporating secular practices to consolidate their power.

As these Hasmonean leaders expanded their territory through military conquests and political alliances, they began adopting practices that blurred the lines between Jewish religious life and Hellenistic influences. This fusion angered groups devoted to strict Torah observance, most notably the Teacher of Righteousness and his followers, who emphasized loyalty to the covenant and condemned political alliances. Psalm 2:2 reflects the dangers of such alliances with worldly authorities: "The kings of the earth set themselves, and the rulers take counsel together, against Jehovah and against his anointed." By aligning with secular rulers, the Hasmoneans jeopardized their religious integrity and opened the door for increasing corruption within the temple system.

The Role of the High Priesthood and Its Shift Toward Political Authority

With the merging of religious and political roles, the position of high priest became more than a spiritual office; it became a seat of political power and influence. Originally designated to represent Israel before Jehovah and offer sacrifices for the nation's sins (Leviticus 16:32-34), the high priesthood under the Hasmoneans morphed into a politically charged role subject to bribery, political appointments, and interference from foreign powers. Unlike previous priestly roles focused solely on spiritual responsibilities, the Hasmonean high priests wielded political influence by acting as rulers over the Jewish nation, thereby blurring sacred and secular lines.

The Prophet Hosea condemned similar religious leaders for their corrupt ambitions: "With their flocks and herds they shall go to seek Jehovah, but they will not find him; he has withdrawn from them. They have dealt faithlessly with Jehovah, for they have borne alien children" (Hosea 5:6-7). This deviation from sacred duty to a political agenda alienated the faithful, such as the Teacher of Righteousness and his community, who sought to maintain a faithful priesthood aligned with Jehovah's covenant. As the high priesthood became increasingly corrupt, a growing division emerged between those loyal to traditional worship and those adapting to new political demands.

The Emergence of Sects: Pharisees, Sadducees, Essenes, and the Qumran Community

The internal tensions of the Second Temple period gave rise to multiple Jewish sects, each with distinct theological and social responses to the temple leadership and political climate. The Pharisees, Sadducees, and Essenes all held differing views regarding adherence to the Law, ritual purity, and the appropriate relationship with foreign authorities. While the Sadducees, typically aligned with the temple and often supportive of the Hasmonean rulers, represented the political and priestly elite, the Pharisees emphasized strict Torah observance among the lay population. They taught in synagogues, focusing on legal interpretations that extended beyond the written Law, which drew criticism from groups like the Teacher of Righteousness.

Ezekiel's warning against priests who serve their own interests rather than Jehovah encapsulates the conflict within the Jewish religious leadership: "Thus says Jehovah God: No foreigner, uncircumcised in heart and flesh, shall enter my sanctuary, including any foreigners who are among the children of Israel" (Ezekiel 44:9). The Teacher of Righteousness and his followers, possibly identifying with the Essenes or a separate group at Qumran, rejected the Sadducees' willingness to compromise on purity laws and political alliances. This community pursued a life of purity, separate from what they viewed as a corrupted religious establishment.

The Qumran Community and Its Opposition to the Hasmonean Leadership

The Qumran community's opposition to the Hasmonean high priests is most evident in the writings of the Dead Sea Scrolls, where the Wicked Priest is condemned as a symbol of temple corruption. In contrast to the Sadducees' acceptance of Hellenistic influences and political power, the Qumran community withdrew into isolation, striving to uphold the covenant's purity and awaiting divine intervention to establish a true theocratic rule. They believed that the high priests' corruption rendered the temple unworthy of Jehovah's presence and, thus, sought spiritual sanctity in their wilderness community, adhering to rigorous purity standards and a strict interpretation of the Law.

Isaiah 1:13-15, which rebukes hollow ritualism, reflects the Qumran community's rejection of the Jerusalem temple's compromised practices: "Bring no more vain offerings; incense is an abomination to me. New moon and Sabbath and the calling of convocations—I cannot endure iniquity and solemn assembly." The Qumran community saw itself as a sanctuary of faithfulness amidst widespread apostasy, committed to preserving Jehovah's law in anticipation of His coming judgment against the corrupt priesthood.

The Teacher of Righteousness vs. the Wicked Priest: A Clash of Ideals

The rivalry between the Teacher of Righteousness and the Wicked Priest epitomized the ideological conflict of the period. While the Teacher of Righteousness emphasized the need for a high priest dedicated to covenantal fidelity and religious purity, the Wicked Priest represented a religious leader who compromised these values for political survival. The Teacher of Righteousness's condemnation of the Wicked Priest aligns with the biblical call for righteous leadership. Psalm 15:1-2 poses the standard for such a leader: "O Jehovah, who shall sojourn in your tent? Who shall dwell on your holy hill? He who walks blamelessly and does what is right and speaks truth in his heart."

This ideological clash reflected broader societal tensions, where some sought to uphold the purity of worship, while others integrated with the prevailing political forces. The Teacher of Righteousness, as seen in the Dead Sea Scrolls, represents those who awaited divine justice, while the Wicked Priest personified a leadership style that prioritized temporal power over eternal principles.

The Impact of Foreign Influence on Religious Leadership

Foreign rule over the Jewish nation, particularly under Hellenistic and later Roman authorities, significantly influenced the nature of the Jewish priesthood and temple leadership. As these foreign powers often exerted control over high priestly appointments, the priesthood became subject to external influences that compromised its sanctity. Unlike leaders like Nehemiah, who actively resisted foreign influence to restore the Law (Nehemiah 13:29), the Hasmonean rulers accepted foreign practices and alliances, leading to a priesthood that, in the view of groups like the Qumran community, had become irreparably tainted.

The Prophet Jeremiah's condemnation of such practices is evident in Jeremiah 2:21, where Jehovah laments the unfaithfulness of His people: "Yet I planted you a choice vine, wholly of pure seed. How then have you turned degenerate and become a wild vine?" The Qumran community saw the temple leadership as a "wild vine" that abandoned its divine purpose, prioritizing foreign alliances over Jehovah's commands.

The political and religious power struggles of the Second Temple period profoundly influenced the dynamics between the Teacher of Righteousness and the Wicked Priest, as well as the formation of various Jewish sects. The Qumran community, rooted in a commitment to Jehovah's covenant, stood in stark opposition to the temple establishment, condemning it for its moral compromises and alliances. These conflicts set the stage for a society divided between those loyal to Jehovah's law and those who sought secular influence, reflecting the enduring tension between faithfulness and political expediency.

CHAPTER 26 The Wicked Priest's Role in the Division of the Jewish Community

The Nature of Divisions in the Jewish Community: Covenant vs. Power

The community divisions during the Second Temple period were deeply rooted in questions of authority, covenantal faithfulness, and the influence of external political pressures. The Wicked Priest's role, as depicted in the Dead Sea Scrolls, was central in exacerbating these divides by aligning with foreign powers and prioritizing political survival over spiritual integrity. By prioritizing power and wealth over covenantal obedience, he became a symbol of the widening rift within the Jewish community. This division aligned him with the Sadducean priesthood, whose compromises stood in stark contrast to groups like the Teacher of Righteousness and the Qumran community, who emphasized purity, scriptural integrity, and anticipation of divine judgment.

Psalm 94:20 illustrates the challenge of religious authorities mingling with secular corruption: "Can wicked rulers be allied with you, those who frame injustice by statute?" The religious compromises of the Wicked Priest and his alliances with Hellenistic rulers represented a betrayal of Israel's unique covenant with Jehovah. His actions contributed to a factionalized religious landscape where groups like the Qumran community rejected the temple leadership, seeking sanctity away from what they deemed a corrupt institution.

The Role of the Wicked Priest in Undermining the Covenant

At the heart of the Jewish community's division was a conflict over the interpretation and application of the Law. The Teacher of Righteousness and his followers viewed the Law as the unchangeable foundation of their covenant with Jehovah, requiring complete faithfulness and adherence. The Wicked Priest, however, approached the Law with a pragmatism that allowed for political adaptability, often bending to Hellenistic influence and corrupt practices to retain his position. This betrayal alienated devout Jews who saw his actions as not only compromising but as a form of idolatry, replacing Jehovah's sovereign Law with foreign values.

Malachi's rebuke of the priests in Malachi 2:7-8 mirrors the community's reaction: "For the lips of a priest should guard knowledge, and people should seek instruction from his mouth, for he is the messenger of Jehovah of hosts. But you have turned aside from the way. You have caused many to stumble by your instruction." The Wicked Priest's tolerance for secular practices led to a split with the Teacher of Righteousness, whose strict adherence to the Law was non-negotiable. This ideological clash marked the inception of two divergent paths within Judaism, where one group pursued purity through separation and the other pursued power through compromise.

Sectarian Responses: The Pharisees, Sadducees, Essenes, and the Qumran Community

The influence of the Wicked Priest's corrupt practices extended beyond the Qumran community, shaping the rise of various sects within Judaism. While the Pharisees advocated for strict observance of the Torah and expansion of oral traditions, the Sadducees aligned closely with the temple and its political alliances. This distinction became especially divisive because the Sadducees, generally aligned with the priesthood, found themselves in a place of privilege within the temple system. The Essenes and the Qumran community, rejecting both the Sadducean and Pharisaic compromises, distanced themselves from the temple altogether, fostering a separatist lifestyle and condemning the temple's leadership for its lack of covenantal fidelity.

Ezekiel's condemnation of corrupt priests underscores the separation that groups like the Qumran community pursued: "Her priests have done violence to my law and have profaned my holy things. They have made no distinction between the holy and the common" (Ezekiel 22:26). The Essenes and the Qumran community saw themselves as the true bearers of Jehovah's covenant, often portraying the Wicked Priest as a usurper whose compromised values led to spiritual unfaithfulness. This rift fostered a deep ideological divide between the temple leadership and those who saw the Law as an unchangeable expression of Jehovah's will.

The Teacher of Righteousness and His Role as a Voice of Faithful Opposition

As the primary adversary of the Wicked Priest, the Teacher of Righteousness became the spiritual leader of the Qumran community and a figurehead for those who felt alienated by the corruption in the temple. The Teacher's dedication to the Law and his rejection of the temple's leadership provided an alternative model of spiritual faithfulness that directly opposed the pragmatism of the Wicked Priest. His teachings emphasized that Israel's identity depended on unyielding commitment to Jehovah's statutes, a stance that clashed with the politically motivated interpretations of the priesthood.

Isaiah 8:20 reflects the Teacher's emphasis on strict adherence to the Law: "To the teaching and to the testimony! If they will not speak according to this word, it is because they have no dawn." The Teacher of Righteousness sought to guide the community by promoting unwavering devotion to Jehovah's commandments, reinforcing the Qumran community's sense of exclusivity as Jehovah's faithful remnant. His opposition to the Wicked Priest reinforced a divide between those who upheld the Law as the ultimate authority and those who saw value in political expediency.

Prophetic Warnings and the Expectation of Divine Judgment

The conflict between the Teacher of Righteousness and the Wicked Priest also embodied an eschatological dimension, where each side anticipated divine intervention to resolve their differences. The Qumran community, guided by the Teacher of Righteousness, interpreted their separation from the temple as a prelude to divine judgment, expecting Jehovah to purify Israel by removing corrupt leaders. Their writings indicate a belief that the Wicked Priest's actions would not go unpunished and that Jehovah would vindicate the faithful by reestablishing a purified priesthood.

The prophet Zechariah speaks of Jehovah's promise to purge corruption: "And on that day, declares Jehovah of hosts, I will cut off the names of the idols from the land, so that they shall be remembered no more" (Zechariah 13:2). This expectation of Jehovah's judgment became central to the Qumran community's worldview, where the Wicked Priest's compromises represented a temporary departure from Jehovah's intended order. The Teacher of Righteousness and his followers awaited a time when the covenant would be restored, and those who upheld its values would be vindicated.

The Wicked Priest's actions played a significant role in dividing the Jewish community of the Second Temple period, pushing devout groups like the Qumran community to reject the established religious leadership. The resulting division fostered the rise of various sects, each responding to the era's challenges in its way. By prioritizing power over covenantal faithfulness, the Wicked Priest catalyzed a schism that underscored the incompatibility between worldly ambition and spiritual integrity.

Edward D. Andrews

CHAPTER 27 The Wicked Priest's Fate: Divine Judgment in the Dead Sea Scrolls

Understanding the Context of Divine Judgment in the Qumran Community

The Dead Sea Scrolls convey a profound theology of divine judgment, woven into the fabric of the Qumran community's worldview. Central to this narrative is the condemnation and eventual judgment of the Wicked Priest, seen as the archenemy of the Teacher of Righteousness and the covenantal community. The scrolls reveal the community's perspective that judgment is not a mere punishment but a decisive intervention by Jehovah to rectify corruption, uphold righteousness, and fulfill the prophetic promises given to Israel.

The Qumran community anticipated a judgment that would not only resolve earthly injustices but also bring about a spiritual purification of Israel. The Wicked Priest's fate illustrates a dual expectation: a temporal judgment reflecting Jehovah's justice on earth and a final judgment that would establish eternal righteousness. This interpretation aligns with passages such as Isaiah 1:27-28, which states, "Zion shall be redeemed by justice, and those in her who repent, by righteousness. But rebels and sinners shall be broken together, and those who forsake Jehovah shall be consumed." The Qumran community believed that Jehovah's judgment would decisively eliminate the influence of those who compromised Israel's purity, with the Wicked Priest being a primary example.

The Wicked Priest as a Symbol of Corruption and Apostasy

The Wicked Priest represents the height of religious corruption, mingling spiritual authority with personal ambition and self-interest. His actions, as chronicled in the Dead Sea Scrolls, reflect a deep-seated defiance of covenantal laws, prioritizing political gain over faithfulness to Jehovah. The Dead Sea Scrolls suggest that his corruption was seen not only in his betrayal of the Qumran community but in his broader failure to uphold the priesthood's sanctity. This transgression is underscored by the warnings in Malachi 2:7-8: "For the lips of a priest should guard knowledge, and people should seek instruction from his mouth, for he is the messenger of Jehovah of hosts. But you have turned aside from the way. You have caused many to stumble by your instruction."

In the Qumran community's view, the Wicked Priest's behavior was an affront to the covenant itself, undermining the Law and leading the people astray. His choices positioned him as an agent of apostasy, one who turned the priestly role into a vehicle for personal benefit rather than spiritual guidance. His fate, therefore, became a crucial aspect of the community's understanding of divine justice. The anticipated judgment upon the Wicked Priest served as a warning to all who would compromise the Law, demonstrating Jehovah's unyielding commitment to purity.

The Mechanics of Divine Retribution: Temporal and Eschatological Dimensions

The judgment anticipated for the Wicked Priest held two primary dimensions: a temporal, earthly retribution and an eschatological, final judgment. The temporal punishment was expected to manifest through tangible consequences—loss of power, illness, or perhaps a violent death—as signs of Jehovah's immediate disapproval. The community likely saw such retribution as Jehovah's intervention to uphold justice on earth. Psalms 37:28 encapsulates this expectation: "For Jehovah loves justice; he will not forsake his saints. They are preserved forever, but the children of the wicked shall be cut off."

This expectation also extended to an eschatological perspective, wherein the final judgment would eradicate all forms of impurity and establish an eternal order. The Qumran texts often speak of a "day of vengeance" when Jehovah would permanently remove the influence of those who had desecrated His covenant. In this sense, the fate of the Wicked Priest became emblematic of Jehovah's promise to establish a future where His law would be upheld without compromise, thus preserving the purity of the faithful remnant.

The Teacher of Righteousness' Role in Declaring Judgment

The Teacher of Righteousness served as the moral and spiritual counterpoint to the Wicked Priest, a figure through whom Jehovah's message of judgment and hope was revealed to the Qumran community. The Teacher not only exemplified covenantal fidelity but also pronounced the impending judgment upon the Wicked Priest. This prophetic role reflects a parallel to the Old Testament prophets, who often called out the failings of Israel's leaders and declared Jehovah's coming judgment against them. Jeremiah 23:1-2 warns, "Woe to the shepherds who destroy and scatter the sheep of my pasture! declares Jehovah." In this way, the Teacher's declarations against the Wicked Priest can be seen as an extension of this prophetic tradition.

The Teacher of Righteousness reinforced the community's hope that Jehovah's judgment would vindicate the faithful and that the Wicked Priest's sins would not go unpunished. His teachings strengthened the community's resolve to endure, believing that Jehovah would ultimately intervene to uphold His covenant. The Teacher's role as a voice of righteousness provided assurance to the community that their suffering and separation were part of Jehovah's plan to refine and preserve a remnant committed to His Law.

The Righteous Remnant: Jehovah's Faithful Witnesses

One of the foundational beliefs within the Qumran community was the concept of a righteous remnant—a group set apart to bear witness to Jehovah's truth and uphold His commandments amid widespread corruption. The remnant served as a testimony against the Wicked Priest, embodying the purity that he had forsaken. This remnant was not merely a social group but a spiritual entity, a gathering of individuals who were to live according to the strictest interpretation of the Law, thus providing a living contrast to the moral decay represented by the Wicked Priest.

This concept finds resonance in Isaiah 10:20-21: "In that day the remnant of Israel and the survivors of the house of Jacob will no more lean on him who struck them, but will lean on Jehovah, the Holy One of Israel, in truth. A remnant will return, the remnant of Jacob, to the mighty God." In the Qumran community's understanding, the Wicked Priest's ultimate fate underscored Jehovah's commitment to preserving this remnant. His judgment upon the Wicked Priest would both purify the priesthood and reaffirm the covenant's sanctity, ensuring that the faithful remnant would carry forward His commandments without compromise.

Prophetic Fulfillment and the Anticipation of a Final Reckoning

The Dead Sea Scrolls reflect the community's conviction that Jehovah's final judgment upon the Wicked Priest would serve as a prophetic fulfillment, signaling the broader judgment awaiting those who defile the covenant. The Qumran community saw themselves as living in a time of anticipation, awaiting Jehovah's intervention to both judge and redeem. The Wicked Priest's fate symbolized a preview of this final reckoning, where Jehovah's righteousness would be fully revealed, and His covenant restored in purity.

This eschatological hope mirrors passages like Daniel 12:2-3, which prophesies a time of resurrection and eternal recompense: "And many of those who sleep in the dust of the earth shall awake, some to everlasting life, and some to shame and everlasting contempt. And those who are wise shall shine like the brightness of the sky above." For the Qumran community, the judgment of the Wicked Priest was a microcosm of the ultimate justice Jehovah would bring upon all nations, separating the faithful from the unfaithful, the pure from the impure.

Theological Significance of the Wicked Priest's Fate

The theological weight of the Wicked Priest's anticipated judgment lay in its affirmation of Jehovah's holiness and the non-negotiable nature of His Law. For the Qumran community, the Wicked Priest's transgressions were not merely personal failings; they were violations that struck at the core of Israel's identity and its covenantal relationship with Jehovah. His punishment was thus seen as necessary to restore Israel's sanctity and reinforce the community's role as the custodians of Jehovah's commandments.

In essence, the fate of the Wicked Priest served as a reminder that no authority, no matter how entrenched, could defy Jehovah's commands with impunity. Ezekiel 18:30 emphasizes this principle: "Therefore I will judge you, O house of Israel, every one according to his ways, declares Jehovah God. Repent and turn from all your transgressions, lest iniquity be your ruin." The Wicked Priest's expected downfall was a powerful testament to Jehovah's unwavering commitment to justice, holiness, and the preservation of a pure community set apart for His purposes.

Conclusion: A Sobering Reminder of Jehovah's Unyielding Justice

The expectation of judgment upon the Wicked Priest became a cornerstone of the Qumran community's faith, embodying their belief that Jehovah would ultimately vindicate the faithful and remove all traces of corruption from Israel's priesthood. This judgment served as both a warning and a source of hope, reinforcing the community's resolve to live in uncompromised adherence to the Law and to anticipate Jehovah's eventual intervention to restore Israel's covenant.

CHAPTER 28 Prophetic Warnings Against the Wicked Priest

The Context of Prophetic Warnings in the Dead Sea Scrolls

The Dead Sea Scrolls portray the Wicked Priest as a figure entrenched in corrupt practices that profoundly impacted the Qumran community's spiritual convictions. The scrolls present prophetic warnings that underscore the seriousness of his transgressions. As an adversary to the Teacher of Righteousness, the Wicked Priest embodies what the community perceived as a deliberate opposition to Jehovah's covenant. Through various prophetic warnings, the scrolls reveal that the consequences awaiting this figure would be severe, driven by divine justice and a desire to preserve the purity of the faithful.

The warnings found within these texts reflect the community's reliance on Jehovah's promises to uphold justice. This is particularly resonant with prophecies from the Hebrew Scriptures, where similar warnings were issued to leaders who defied Jehovah's laws. For instance, in Jeremiah 23:1-2, Jehovah declares, "Woe to the shepherds who destroy and scatter the sheep of my pasture!... you have not attended to them. Behold, I will attend to you for your evil deeds." These passages help illuminate the perspective of the Qumran community, which viewed the Wicked Priest as deserving of the same reproof and accountability as those whom Jehovah condemned in ancient times.

Identifying the Nature of the Wicked Priest's Transgressions

The Dead Sea Scrolls describe the Wicked Priest's violations in both ethical and religious terms, indicating a profound deviation from the values upheld by the Teacher of Righteousness. These texts illustrate that his actions were not merely personal failures but represented a systemic betrayal of the priestly role, which required adherence to Jehovah's laws. The Wicked Priest's behaviors—self-interest, greed, and abuse of authority—position him as a stark contrast to the Teacher's emphasis on righteousness and humility.

In the Habakkuk Pesher, the Wicked Priest's transgressions are underscored by accusations of bloodshed, greed, and hypocrisy. His conduct is condemned for desecrating sacred responsibilities, suggesting an abandonment of the holiness that Jehovah required from Israel's leaders. The prophetic warnings against him align with rebukes found in Ezekiel 34:2-4, where Jehovah condemns Israel's leaders who "have not strengthened the weak, healed the sick, bound up the injured, brought back the strayed, or sought the lost, but with force and harshness you have ruled them."

The Role of Prophetic Fulfillment in the Community's Warnings

The prophetic warnings conveyed through the Dead Sea Scrolls function not only as declarations of impending judgment but as assurances to the faithful that Jehovah's promises would be fulfilled. In the context of the Qumran community, these warnings were instrumental in fostering hope and resilience. They assured the community that, despite the Wicked Priest's defiance, Jehovah would eventually establish justice. This theme of prophetic fulfillment resonates with the broader biblical narrative, where prophetic warnings often serve to reinforce Jehovah's unchanging standards.

In Isaiah 55:11, Jehovah declares, "So shall my word be that goes out from my mouth; it shall not return to me empty, but it shall accomplish that which I purpose." This promise underscores the

Qumran community's belief that the judgment against the Wicked Priest would come to pass as an unalterable fulfillment of Jehovah's word. For the Qumran community, these prophetic warnings reinforced the inevitability of divine retribution, offering reassurance that their suffering at the hands of the Wicked Priest would be vindicated by Jehovah's justice.

Comparing Prophetic Warnings in the Hebrew Scriptures and the Dead Sea Scrolls

The prophetic warnings against the Wicked Priest in the Dead Sea Scrolls parallel the rebukes given to corrupt leaders throughout the Hebrew Scriptures. Leaders such as Ahab and the high priests of Israel, who misused their power and led the people into idolatry, were similarly condemned by Jehovah's prophets. For instance, in 1 Kings 21:20-21, Elijah confronts Ahab with a harsh rebuke, declaring Jehovah's intention to "consume" him due to his corruption and injustice. This comparison deepens the understanding of how the Qumran community viewed the Wicked Priest, interpreting his actions as equally grievous and worthy of Jehovah's retribution.

The scrolls emphasize that the Wicked Priest's fate would be similar to that of these past figures. By doing so, the Qumran community connected their present struggle with the historical faithfulness of Jehovah to judge leaders who violated His commands. This connection fortified the community's confidence in divine justice and reinforced their separation from what they perceived as a corrupt priesthood, aligning themselves with the prophetic traditions that Jehovah would ultimately act to restore purity.

The Prophetic Warnings as a Call to Endurance for the Qumran Community

The Dead Sea Scrolls not only pronounce warnings against the Wicked Priest but also serve as a call for the Qumran community to endure amid adversity. This endurance was seen as both an act of faithfulness and a testimony to Jehovah's holiness. The prophetic messages directed toward the Wicked Priest were a reminder to the community that Jehovah's timing in executing judgment was perfect and that their steadfastness would be rewarded.

Habakkuk 2:3 echoes this sentiment: "For still the vision awaits its appointed time; it hastens to the end—it will not lie. If it seems slow, wait for it; it will surely come; it will not delay." For the Qumran community, this waiting period was an exercise in faith and trust in Jehovah's justice. By maintaining their commitment to Jehovah's commands, they positioned themselves as the faithful remnant who would witness the Wicked Priest's ultimate downfall and the vindication of their covenantal faith.

The Consequences of Ignoring Jehovah's Warnings

The Dead Sea Scrolls present a stern view of the consequences for those who ignore Jehovah's warnings, drawing on the experiences of Israel's leaders who failed to heed prophetic counsel. The scrolls imply that the Wicked Priest's resistance to prophetic warnings did not negate their eventual fulfillment but rather hastened his judgment. This understanding aligns with Jehovah's rebukes in Zechariah 7:11-12: "But they refused to pay attention and turned a stubborn shoulder… Therefore, great anger came from Jehovah of hosts."

The Wicked Priest's disregard for Jehovah's authority intensified the community's conviction that his judgment was justified. His actions were seen as a blatant disregard for the holiness of Jehovah's law, and his refusal to repent further solidified his fate. This served as a stark warning to the community and reinforced the Qumran community's commitment to remain vigilant and attentive to Jehovah's instructions.

The Dual Role of Prophetic Warnings: Judgment and Redemption

The prophetic warnings against the Wicked Priest reveal a dual purpose within the Dead Sea Scrolls. While primarily directed at condemning the Wicked Priest's actions, these warnings also served as reminders of Jehovah's overarching plan for redemption. The Qumran community saw themselves as part of this divine plan, positioned to witness the restoration of Israel's covenant with Jehovah. The community's hope was that, through the judgment of the Wicked Priest, Jehovah would restore purity to the priesthood and uphold the sanctity of His covenant.

This theme resonates with Joel 2:13-14, where Jehovah calls His people to "return to [Him] with all [their] heart," assuring them that "He relents over disaster." For the Qumran community, the Wicked Priest's judgment was not solely punitive but part of Jehovah's redemptive process, a necessary step in restoring the priesthood and renewing His covenant with the faithful remnant.

The Wicked Priest's Judgment as a Testament to Jehovah's Justice

The prophetic warnings against the Wicked Priest in the Dead Sea Scrolls illustrate that Jehovah's justice is both certain and thorough. His judgment serves as a testament to His unchanging standards, reinforcing the Qumran community's confidence in Jehovah's commitment to preserve His covenant. The Wicked Priest's impending judgment was seen not only as an act of retribution but as a declaration that Jehovah would not tolerate the perversion of His law by those entrusted to uphold it.

In Deuteronomy 32:4, Jehovah is described as "a God of faithfulness and without iniquity, just and upright." The Qumran community believed that these qualities would manifest in the judgment upon the Wicked Priest, who had betrayed the covenantal responsibilities of his position. Jehovah's justice, as presented in the Dead Sea Scrolls, affirms His dedication to upholding righteousness and serves as a reminder that those who deviate from His commands will ultimately face divine retribution.

Conclusion: The Enduring Impact of Prophetic Warnings in the Dead Sea Scrolls

The prophetic warnings against the Wicked Priest encapsulate the Dead Sea Scrolls' message of divine justice, a justice that defends the faithful and condemns corruption. Through these warnings, the

Qumran community saw a future in which Jehovah's authority would be reaffirmed and His people restored. The Wicked Priest's fate, as foretold in these prophetic declarations, stands as a testament to Jehovah's holiness and His unwavering dedication to those who uphold His covenant.

CHAPTER 29 The Wicked Priest as a Symbol of Corruption and Apostasy

The Wicked Priest as the Embodiment of Corruption

The Wicked Priest, as depicted in the Dead Sea Scrolls, serves as a striking figure symbolizing the depths of corruption and apostasy. His portrayal offers a cautionary narrative about the dangers that come from a deviation from divine principles, revealing the consequences when spiritual leaders forsake their duties to Jehovah. The texts repeatedly emphasize that his actions were not only individual failings but reflective of a systemic decay infiltrating Israel's religious institutions. The figure of the Wicked Priest encapsulates traits of material greed, disregard for the covenant, and the prioritization of personal ambition over godly devotion, all of which made him a formidable adversary to the Teacher of Righteousness and his followers.

The Dead Sea Scrolls suggest that the Wicked Priest's transgressions were not merely political missteps but profound spiritual failings. His actions represent the antithesis of the righteous conduct that the Qumran community valued. For instance, in the *Pesher Habakkuk*, a commentary on the Book of Habakkuk, the Wicked Priest is condemned for accumulating wealth through exploitative practices and for disrespecting sacred duties. His conduct is reminiscent of the behavior of corrupt rulers in the Hebrew Scriptures, such as those described in Ezekiel 34:2-3, where Jehovah rebukes Israel's leaders for "feeding themselves" rather than tending to the flock. This rebuke underscores the expectation of moral integrity in those leading Jehovah's people, an expectation the Wicked Priest ultimately forsook.

185

Apostasy as the Core of the Wicked Priest's Character

The term "apostasy" denotes a willful abandonment of faith and a deviation from Jehovah's covenantal requirements. The Dead Sea Scrolls highlight the Wicked Priest's actions as a grave departure from these expectations. His willingness to compromise sacred principles for personal gain symbolizes an apostasy that not only impacted him but also contributed to the spiritual degradation of those under his influence. The texts portray him as not merely a passive participant in religious affairs but as an active agent of deviation from Jehovah's commands, making his role all the more insidious.

In the Qumran community's interpretation, the Wicked Priest's rejection of the covenant parallels the broader theme of apostasy seen in other historical accounts. His disregard for covenantal fidelity calls to mind the warning in Deuteronomy 13:4-5, where Jehovah commands His people to "walk after Jehovah your God and fear him and keep his commandments and obey his voice." The consequence for leading others astray was severe in Israel's history, and the Dead Sea Scrolls extend this understanding to the Wicked Priest, whose influence led many to compromise their dedication to Jehovah.

The Contrast Between the Teacher of Righteousness and the Wicked Priest

The stark contrast between the Teacher of Righteousness and the Wicked Priest underscores the community's perception of true and false spiritual leadership. While the Teacher of Righteousness adhered to Jehovah's laws and promoted a lifestyle aligned with scriptural teachings, the Wicked Priest pursued self-interest and neglected the ethical mandates of his position. The Teacher of Righteousness stood as a beacon of faithfulness, while the Wicked Priest embodied the betrayal of these foundational values.

This contrast reflects a broader biblical pattern where Jehovah establishes faithful leaders in opposition to those who forsake their duties. For instance, Moses confronted the idolatry of Israel with steadfast dedication to Jehovah's commands, even as others were tempted by disobedience (Exodus 32:26-28). Similarly, the Qumran community viewed the Teacher of Righteousness as someone standing firm against the corrupting influences represented by the Wicked Priest, drawing a line between those who honored Jehovah and those who fell into apostasy.

The Role of Wealth and Power in Corruption

One of the most striking aspects of the Wicked Priest's character is his attachment to wealth and power, which served as primary motivators for his apostasy. The Dead Sea Scrolls depict him as a leader who prioritized material gain over spiritual integrity. His accumulation of wealth is portrayed as indicative of his moral decay and a clear violation of the humility expected of a priestly role. The Teacher of Righteousness, in contrast, represented a life devoted to spiritual pursuits, placing obedience to Jehovah above all earthly ambitions.

The scripture in 1 Timothy 6:10, which states, "For the love of money is a root of all kinds of evil," resonates with the portrayal of the Wicked Priest. His love for material wealth undermined his commitment to Jehovah and led him into corruption. In the Dead Sea Scrolls, this love for wealth is not seen merely as a personal failing but as a characteristic that rendered him unworthy of his office. His actions served as a cautionary example of how unchecked desires can lead one to forsake Jehovah's commandments.

Apostasy and Divine Judgment in the Hebrew Scriptures

The Dead Sea Scrolls suggest that the Wicked Priest's fate was sealed by his choices, drawing from themes of divine judgment found throughout the Hebrew Scriptures. His apostasy and betrayal of Jehovah's covenant inevitably led to his downfall, reflecting the biblical principle that leaders who deviate from divine mandates invite judgment upon themselves. This concept is emphasized in passages like Hosea 4:6, where Jehovah warns, "My people are destroyed for lack of knowledge; because you have rejected knowledge, I reject you from being a priest to me." The Wicked Priest's disregard for knowledge and devotion to Jehovah's covenant placed him in a position of rejection and condemnation.

The Qumran community saw these principles in action through the fate they believed awaited the Wicked Priest. His life exemplified the repercussions of abandoning the covenant and underscored the justice inherent in Jehovah's response to such actions. The Dead Sea Scrolls provide a narrative in which the Wicked Priest's ultimate judgment serves as both a vindication of Jehovah's justice and a warning to others who might similarly fall into apostasy.

The Symbolic Significance of the Wicked Priest's Downfall

The Qumran community interpreted the Wicked Priest's downfall as more than a historical event; it served as a powerful symbol of Jehovah's intolerance for corruption within His people. His eventual fate acted as a testament to the enduring righteousness that Jehovah expects from those in leadership. Just as the Teacher of Righteousness exemplified the righteous path, the Wicked Priest embodied the consequences of rejecting that path.

The community's understanding of this downfall mirrors the message in Proverbs 11:5, which states, "The righteousness of the blameless keeps his way straight, but the wicked falls by his own wickedness." The Wicked Priest's downfall was seen as a fulfillment of this principle, with his own corrupt practices bringing about his end. The Dead Sea Scrolls thus reinforce the message that faithfulness to Jehovah's standards brings life and security, while deviation from these standards results in judgment.

Apostasy's Impact on the Faithful Remnant

While the Wicked Priest symbolized corruption and apostasy, the Qumran community viewed themselves as the faithful remnant, striving to uphold Jehovah's standards amidst widespread spiritual decay. They believed that their commitment to the covenant distinguished them from the apostate practices associated with the

Wicked Priest. The community's strict adherence to ritual purity, scriptural study, and covenantal observance represented their dedication to living as a contrast to the corruption exemplified by the Wicked Priest.

The concept of a faithful remnant is deeply rooted in the Hebrew Scriptures, where Jehovah preserves a group who remain loyal despite widespread apostasy. In 1 Kings 19:18, Jehovah reassures Elijah, saying, "Yet I will leave seven thousand in Israel, all the knees that have not bowed to Baal." The Qumran community saw themselves as this loyal group, set apart by their faithfulness and commitment to Jehovah's laws, even when those in positions of power, like the Wicked Priest, had forsaken those laws.

Lessons on Apostasy and Leadership for Future Generations

The Dead Sea Scrolls' portrayal of the Wicked Priest provides timeless lessons about the dangers of apostasy and the responsibilities that come with spiritual leadership. His story serves as a warning to those who hold positions of influence within Jehovah's community, emphasizing the necessity of integrity, humility, and fidelity to divine principles. The Wicked Priest's life demonstrates that power and prestige are meaningless if they are not accompanied by a sincere commitment to Jehovah's standards.

This lesson echoes the biblical principle found in Micah 6:8, where it is written, "He has told you, O man, what is good; and what does Jehovah require of you but to do justice, and to love kindness, and to walk humbly with your God?" The Wicked Priest's failure to embody these qualities led to his downfall, reinforcing the idea that true leadership within Jehovah's people must be grounded in righteousness.

Conclusion: The Enduring Significance of the Wicked Priest as a Symbol of Apostasy

The character of the Wicked Priest, as presented in the Dead Sea Scrolls, represents the ultimate consequences of forsaking Jehovah's commandments for personal gain. His life stands as a symbol of what happens when leaders abandon their responsibilities and prioritize worldly desires over their devotion to Jehovah. The prophetic warnings, the Teacher of Righteousness's opposition, and the ultimate judgment all serve as reminders of Jehovah's expectations for those who are called to guide His people. In this way, the Wicked Priest's legacy is a cautionary tale for all who seek to serve Jehovah, underscoring the paramount importance of faithfulness, humility, and unwavering commitment to the covenant.

CHAPTER 30 The Wicked Priest and Apocalyptic Judgment

The Apocalyptic Context of the Dead Sea Scrolls

In the context of the Dead Sea Scrolls, apocalyptic judgment is a significant theme, particularly regarding figures of corruption and opposition, like the Wicked Priest. This figure embodies the antithesis of the Teacher of Righteousness and stands as a symbol of everything that threatens covenantal purity and devotion to Jehovah. The Dead Sea Scrolls describe the Wicked Priest in terms that align with other biblical depictions of those who forsake God's ways. The apocalyptic literature within the Scrolls emphasizes Jehovah's final judgment as a means to restore holiness and execute justice against those who have forsaken His covenant.

The idea of apocalyptic judgment reflects the view held by the Qumran community that God would intervene in human affairs to establish justice and punish the wicked. As prophesied in texts such as the *Pesher Habakkuk* (1QpHab), the fate of the Wicked Priest is laid out as a demonstration of God's active judgment against corruption and unfaithfulness. By viewing the actions of the Wicked Priest as a betrayal, the community reinforced its belief in the apocalyptic retribution awaiting all who aligned themselves against God's truth.

The Wicked Priest as an Object of Divine Wrath

The Dead Sea Scrolls present the Wicked Priest not only as a corrupt leader but as an adversary to God's covenantal expectations. His life and actions illustrate the characteristics of apostasy and arrogance that provoke God's wrath. Through prophetic interpretation, the community depicted him as a man who pursued personal gain at the cost of God's sacred trust, likening him to figures of infamy within Israel's history who fell under God's judgment. The Wicked Priest, thus, stands in contrast to faithful servants like Moses, who upheld God's laws and mediated on behalf of the people.

The Book of Habakkuk serves as a foundational prophetic text in the Scrolls, and its interpretation in the *Pesher* provides insight into the Qumran community's view of divine justice. In Habakkuk 2:4, Jehovah declares, "The righteous shall live by his faith." In this passage, the community found justification for their belief that the righteous, represented by the Teacher of Righteousness, would ultimately be vindicated by God. Conversely, the Wicked Priest, who lacked faithfulness and betrayed the covenant, became a prime target for Jehovah's righteous indignation.

Apocalyptic Imagery in the Dead Sea Scrolls

The apocalyptic descriptions in the Dead Sea Scrolls portray a vivid picture of the fate awaiting the Wicked Priest. The Qumran community expected divine intervention that would bring an end to the current era of corruption, ushering in a period of restoration and divine authority. The Scrolls employ symbolic language, portraying the Wicked Priest's downfall as inevitable under God's plan for justice. The imagery emphasizes a direct, supernatural act of God, leaving no room for escape for those who oppose Him.

In these texts, the Qumran community parallels the fate of the Wicked Priest with the broader biblical warnings against apostasy and rebellion. This perspective is similar to the descriptions of judgment in the prophets. For instance, in Isaiah 13:11, Jehovah declares, "I will punish the world for its evil, and the wicked for their iniquity." Such language resonates with the apocalyptic declarations found in the Dead Sea Scrolls, particularly concerning the Wicked Priest, as the community anticipated the final intervention of God to cleanse His people from corruption.

The Symbolic Role of Judgment in Purifying God's People

For the Qumran community, apocalyptic judgment was not merely retributive but also purifying. By bringing judgment against figures like the Wicked Priest, God would remove the corruption that had infiltrated His people, setting the stage for a renewed relationship with the faithful remnant. This purifying judgment was central to the Qumran worldview, as they saw themselves as part of the remnant chosen to maintain the covenant in a time of widespread apostasy. The Wicked Priest, as a symbol of impurity and moral decay, was destined for destruction, which would signal the cleansing of Israel and the restoration of true worship.

The Dead Sea Scrolls' view of this purifying process reflects biblical themes of divine refining, as seen in Malachi 3:2-3, which states that Jehovah "will sit as a refiner and purifier of silver, and he will purify the sons of Levi and refine them like gold and silver." The Qumran community believed that God's judgment upon figures like the Wicked Priest was necessary to achieve this purification, preserving the integrity of God's people and the covenant.

The Fate of the Wicked Priest and the Final Judgment

The expectation of a final, decisive judgment reflects the apocalyptic worldview of the Qumran community. They believed that the culmination of this divine intervention would be the complete removal of unrighteousness from among Jehovah's people. The Wicked Priest's fate is thus presented as both a specific act of judgment and a precursor to the ultimate fulfillment of God's plan. In the Dead Sea Scrolls, the condemnation of the Wicked Priest aligns with the prophetic expectation of judgment upon those who lead God's people astray.

Passages like Isaiah 66:15-16 portray this final judgment, stating, "For behold, Jehovah will come in fire, and his chariots like the whirlwind, to render his anger in fury, and his rebuke with flames of fire. For by fire will Jehovah enter into judgment, and by his sword, with all flesh." The Qumran community's anticipation of such an event underscores their understanding that figures like the Wicked Priest were destined for judgment, aligning with the divine plan to eradicate all sources of impurity and corruption.

The Eschatological Hope of the Faithful Community

The apocalyptic judgment that awaited the Wicked Priest also reinforced the Qumran community's hope in God's promises. They held to the belief that Jehovah's ultimate judgment would restore justice, allowing the faithful to dwell securely under His reign. The Teacher of Righteousness, representing the righteous remnant, embodied this hope, serving as a model for the community's perseverance and loyalty to Jehovah. This expectation of divine intervention offered the community reassurance that their struggles were temporary and that justice would be accomplished in God's timing.

The apostle Peter echoes a similar sentiment in 2 Peter 3:13, affirming that "we are waiting for new heavens and a new earth in which righteousness dwells." The Qumran community's anticipation of judgment against the Wicked Priest aligns with this hope for a renewed order, where Jehovah's standards of righteousness would prevail over corruption and apostasy. Thus, the fate of the Wicked Priest became a reminder to the community of their own calling to maintain purity in anticipation of Jehovah's deliverance.

Conclusion: Apocalyptic Judgment as the Fulfillment of Divine Justice

In examining the fate of the Wicked Priest through the lens of apocalyptic judgment, the Dead Sea Scrolls provide a comprehensive portrayal of Jehovah's unwavering commitment to uphold His covenant. This judgment reflects the enduring principle that God will act to eliminate corruption and preserve a remnant devoted to His commands. For the Qumran community, the Wicked Priest's downfall served as both a warning and a reassurance, affirming that, in the end, God's justice would prevail, securing a purified people faithful to His covenant.

CHAPTER 31 Comparing the Wicked Priest to Biblical Adversaries

The Wicked Priest and His Role in Apostasy

In understanding the Wicked Priest as portrayed in the Dead Sea Scrolls, we observe a direct link between his conduct and that of biblical figures associated with defiance against God's covenant. The Wicked Priest embodies corruption and betrayal, standing in stark contrast to the Teacher of Righteousness, whom the Qumran community revered for his faithfulness to God's standards. The figure of the Wicked Priest parallels several adversarial characters in the Bible, where individuals rise in opposition to God's will, whether by introducing idolatry, misleading the people, or using their position of authority for personal gain.

The Qumran community's portrayal of the Wicked Priest fits within this tradition of apostasy, and he is characterized as a leader who subverts the covenant, betrays the community, and incurs God's wrath. This role underscores the broader theme within the Dead Sea Scrolls: God's intolerance for leaders who forsake the divine commandments, as reflected in Proverbs 28:4, where it states, "Those who forsake the law praise the wicked, but those who keep the law strive against them." Thus, the Wicked Priest's actions align him with those condemned in Scripture, highlighting a continuity in how disobedience and misuse of authority are viewed by the devout.

The Wicked Priest and King Saul: A Case of Betrayal and Rejection

One apt comparison can be made between the Wicked Priest and King Saul. Saul's kingship, while initially marked by promise, quickly turned toward defiance and disregard for God's commands. Saul's disobedience, specifically his failure to completely destroy the Amalekites as instructed (1 Samuel 15:9-11), revealed his prioritization of personal ambition over adherence to God's instructions. Consequently, Jehovah rejected Saul, leading the prophet Samuel to rebuke him, stating, "Because you have rejected the word of Jehovah, he has also rejected you from being king" (1 Samuel 15:23).

In a similar vein, the Wicked Priest, holding a position of religious authority, allowed personal ambitions to overshadow his duty to uphold the covenant. The Qumran texts portray him as indulging in activities that defile his office, ultimately forsaking the covenant in favor of self-interest. Just as Saul's failure to respect his divine mandate led to his downfall, the Wicked Priest's neglect of his responsibilities and covenantal duties resulted in a divinely ordained judgment, thus echoing the biblical principle that authority must be exercised in alignment with God's standards.

The Wicked Priest and Ahab: The Promotion of Idolatry and Apostasy

Another striking parallel can be observed between the Wicked Priest and King Ahab. Ahab's reign was infamous for its open endorsement of idolatry and Baal worship, which led to significant corruption among the Israelites. Ahab's marriage to Jezebel, who actively promoted the worship of Baal, led him to abandon Jehovah's ways entirely. 1 Kings 21:25-26 illustrates Ahab's legacy, noting, "There was none who sold himself to do what was evil in the sight of Jehovah like Ahab, whom Jezebel his wife incited. He acted very abominably in going after idols."

Similar to Ahab, the Wicked Priest is portrayed in the Dead Sea Scrolls as an individual who brought corruption into what should have been a holy office. His actions, rooted in self-interest and neglect for covenantal purity, represent a turning away from God's commandments. The Qumran community saw him as a figure who not only betrayed his calling but also led others astray through his corrupt leadership, much like Ahab, whose reign contributed to Israel's spiritual decline. The Dead Sea Scrolls' apocalyptic expectations include a retribution that will cleanse Israel of such corruption, thereby fulfilling the prophetic rebuke against those who, like Ahab, led Israel into sin.

The Wicked Priest and Judas Iscariot: Betrayal of the Faithful

The betrayal of the Teacher of Righteousness by the Wicked Priest brings to mind the betrayal of Jesus by Judas Iscariot. Judas, who was initially counted among the apostles, betrayed Jesus for personal gain, ultimately forsaking his relationship with his master for thirty pieces of silver. This betrayal was not merely an act of personal disloyalty but a severe violation of trust and an affront to God's redemptive plan. In Matthew 26:24, Jesus reflects on Judas's act, stating, "The Son of Man goes as it is written of him, but woe to that man by whom the Son of Man is betrayed! It would have been better for that man if he had not been born."

Likewise, the Wicked Priest's betrayal of the Teacher of Righteousness in the Qumran community represents a profound breach of trust. As one who had assumed a position meant to safeguard the spiritual integrity of the community, the Wicked Priest's actions exemplify the same duplicity and disregard for the covenant as seen in Judas. The betrayal not only symbolizes personal failure but reflects a broader theological statement: betrayal by those closest to the faith brings upon them the severest of judgments, affirming the community's view that God will not tolerate such treachery.

The Wicked Priest and Korah: A Revolt Against Divine Authority

In the book of Numbers, Korah, along with his followers, openly challenged Moses' divinely appointed leadership, seeking to usurp authority over Israel. Korah's rebellion was not just an act of disobedience but a direct affront to Jehovah's chosen representative. Numbers 16:3 records the audacity of Korah's challenge: "They assembled themselves together against Moses and against Aaron and said to them, 'You have gone too far! For all in the congregation are holy, every one of them, and Jehovah is among them.'" The result of this rebellion was swift and decisive, as Jehovah caused the earth to open and swallow Korah and his followers.

Similarly, the Wicked Priest's actions can be seen as a challenge to the spiritual authority established within the Qumran community. By opposing the Teacher of Righteousness and attempting to undermine the community's covenantal integrity, the Wicked Priest mirrored Korah's defiance. The Qumran community saw the Wicked Priest's opposition as not merely a personal grievance but as a challenge to God's order and authority, warranting the same kind of divine retribution that Korah faced. The parallels with Korah's rebellion reinforce the message that those who defy divine authority and seek personal power within a sacred community ultimately face destruction.

The Wicked Priest and Hophni and Phinehas: Profaning the Priesthood

The biblical figures of Hophni and Phinehas, the sons of Eli, serve as another fitting comparison. These priests abused their positions by engaging in immoral and corrupt practices, exploiting their role for selfish gain. 1 Samuel 2:12-17 describes their conduct, noting that they "did not know Jehovah" and that they treated the offerings of Jehovah with contempt. Their actions led to God's judgment, resulting in their untimely deaths as a sign of divine displeasure.

The Dead Sea Scrolls similarly portray the Wicked Priest as one who profaned his office, engaging in practices that compromised the sanctity of the priesthood. His failure to uphold the holiness expected of a priest aligned him with figures like Hophni and Phinehas, whose contempt for their duties brought divine judgment upon them. The Qumran community likely viewed the Wicked Priest's actions through this lens, understanding his corruption as a breach of the covenant that would inevitably provoke God's wrath.

Conclusion: The Continuity of Apostasy and Divine Judgment

Throughout biblical history, figures who misuse their authority or openly defy God's commandments face a consistent theme of judgment. The Wicked Priest, as portrayed in the Dead Sea Scrolls, joins this list of adversarial characters whose actions not only lead to personal ruin but also underscore the importance of faithfulness to the covenant. In each of these comparisons—Saul, Ahab, Judas, Korah, Hophni, and Phinehas—there exists a clear pattern: those who forsake God's established order invite divine judgment, serving as warnings for future generations.

CHAPTER 32 The Conflict Between the Wicked Priest and the Teacher of Righteousness

The Origins of the Conflict: Divergent Paths in Spiritual Leadership

The Dead Sea Scrolls depict the clash between the Teacher of Righteousness and the Wicked Priest as a deep spiritual and theological conflict. This confrontation goes beyond mere personal differences; it reflects two diametrically opposed views on religious integrity and covenantal loyalty. The Teacher of Righteousness, as a figurehead of devotion to the covenant, is depicted as guiding his community according to the principles of holiness, obedience, and humility before Jehovah. By contrast, the Wicked Priest, in his pursuits, is characterized by corruption, self-interest, and a flagrant disregard for the covenant's moral and spiritual obligations.

The scrolls suggest that this conflict did not arise out of one isolated incident but was rooted in fundamental theological and ethical differences. While the Teacher of Righteousness adhered strictly to the covenantal laws and the pursuit of holiness, the Wicked Priest prioritized personal power and worldly influence, disregarding the sanctity of his office. This divergence is illustrated in the texts by the Wicked Priest's actions, which demonstrate his descent from godly values toward practices that corrupted the priesthood and harmed the community's spiritual wellbeing. Proverbs 29:2 captures the essence of this dynamic: "When the righteous increase, the people rejoice, but when the wicked rule, the people groan." This proverb encapsulates the distress experienced by the Qumran community as they witnessed the Wicked Priest's actions.

The Nature of Their Disputes: Doctrinal Integrity Versus Religious Compromise

A central theme of the conflict lies in the adherence to doctrinal purity versus accommodation with worldly values. The Teacher of Righteousness upheld a strict interpretation of the law, emphasizing the need for purity and righteousness as foundational to Israel's relationship with Jehovah. This view aligned with passages like Deuteronomy 10:12-13, which stress the call for Israel to "fear Jehovah your God, to walk in all his ways, to love him, to serve Jehovah your God with all your heart and with all your soul, and to keep the commandments and statutes of Jehovah."

In contrast, the Wicked Priest represents a willingness to compromise these doctrines in pursuit of political and material gain. His behavior echoes the pattern of leaders throughout biblical history who, for the sake of expediency, deviated from God's commands. The Qumran community's texts criticize the Wicked Priest for his indifference to maintaining the purity of the priesthood, suggesting that he exploited his office for personal advancement, thus betraying the covenant and disregarding the weight of the sacred responsibilities it entailed.

The scrolls portray the Teacher's staunch commitment to the law as a direct rebuke to the Wicked Priest's conduct. This distinction illustrates a recurrent biblical theme where false leaders emerge as corrupting influences, leading people away from true worship. For example, Malachi 2:7-8 condemns the priests of Israel for causing many to stumble through their failure to "preserve knowledge" and remain faithful to their office. The conflict between the Teacher and the Wicked Priest, then, serves as a reiteration of this same caution against deviation from God's covenant.

The Personal Persecution of the Teacher: Suffering as a Mark of Faithfulness

A striking element of this rivalry is the personal suffering endured by the Teacher of Righteousness, who experienced oppression and persecution from the Wicked Priest. This persecution reflects the broader biblical principle that those who seek to uphold God's standards often encounter opposition from those who stand in defiance of them. The Teacher's suffering is not depicted as a result of personal flaws but as a direct consequence of his commitment to the truth of the covenant, aligning him with the tradition of righteous individuals who faced trials for their faithfulness. Psalm 34:19 aptly reflects this, stating, "Many are the afflictions of the righteous, but Jehovah delivers him out of them all."

The Qumran community, identifying closely with the Teacher's experiences, interpreted his sufferings as evidence of his righteousness and fidelity to the covenant. They viewed him as a righteous figure akin to the prophets who endured persecution for proclaiming Jehovah's will. His experiences mirror those of figures like Jeremiah, who faced hostility for condemning the corrupt practices of the religious leaders of his time (Jeremiah 20:1-2). The Teacher's endurance of suffering thus serves as a testament to his unwavering loyalty to God's standards, reinforcing the community's conviction that righteousness may come at a cost but will ultimately receive divine vindication.

The Wicked Priest's Betrayal and Its Consequences

The Wicked Priest's betrayal is described with a sense of finality, indicating a complete departure from the covenant and a severe breach of his role. The Teacher of Righteousness likely viewed this betrayal as symptomatic of a larger spiritual malaise affecting Israel's leadership. This aligns with the portrayal of treacherous leaders in passages like Ezekiel 22:26, where Jehovah condemns the priests who "do violence to my law and profane my holy things. They make no distinction between the holy and the common." Such leaders were seen as undermining the covenant by leading the people into defilement, forsaking their role as mediators of God's holiness.

In betraying the Teacher and, by extension, the covenantal principles he represented, the Wicked Priest became a symbol of apostasy within the Qumran community. His actions not only constituted personal failure but also had communal implications, as he misled others and contributed to a broader pattern of spiritual decline.

The scrolls suggest that his betrayal brought divine retribution, an inevitable consequence of violating the covenant. This theme echoes passages like Psalm 37:38, which states, "But transgressors shall be altogether destroyed; the future of the wicked shall be cut off." The Qumran texts thus present the Wicked Priest's downfall as a fulfillment of divine justice, affirming the certainty of God's judgment against those who forsake His commandments.

The Symbolism of Darkness and Light: Spiritual Warfare in the Dead Sea Scrolls

The conflict between the Teacher of Righteousness and the Wicked Priest is also expressed symbolically as a struggle between light and darkness, a motif prevalent in the Dead Sea Scrolls. This symbolism encapsulates the theological divide between adherence to God's commandments (light) and the embrace of sin and corruption (darkness). The Teacher of Righteousness is associated with the "sons of light," those committed to Jehovah and His covenant, while the Wicked Priest is aligned with the "sons of darkness," representing forces opposed to God's purposes. This imagery of light and darkness is reinforced by passages such as Isaiah 5:20, which warns, "Woe to those who call evil good and good evil, who put darkness for light and light for darkness."

By framing their struggle in terms of spiritual warfare, the Qumran community viewed the conflict as an extension of the broader cosmic battle between righteousness and wickedness. They believed that the Wicked Priest, in aligning with darkness, was not merely an adversary to the Teacher but a direct opponent to Jehovah's purposes. This understanding of their conflict intensified the community's resolve to uphold the teachings of the Teacher of Righteousness, whom they saw as a beacon of light amidst a world of increasing moral decay.

The Vindication of the Teacher and the Demise of the Wicked Priest

The Dead Sea Scrolls reflect a belief in the ultimate vindication of the Teacher of Righteousness and the punishment of the Wicked

Priest. The Qumran community held that Jehovah would eventually bring justice, exposing and punishing those who desecrate the covenant. Psalm 37:6 provides a fitting expression of this hope, declaring, "He will bring forth your righteousness as the light, and your justice as the noonday." This confidence in divine vindication underscored the community's conviction that the Wicked Priest's actions would not go unpunished and that Jehovah would ultimately affirm the righteousness of the Teacher.

The Wicked Priest's anticipated downfall is depicted as a divine response to his corruption and betrayal. The Qumran texts suggest that his actions would not only lead to his personal ruin but also serve as a warning to others. Much like Hophni and Phinehas, who faced judgment for profaning the priesthood, the Wicked Priest's demise reinforces the principle that leaders who abuse their roles will face severe consequences. This theme of divine justice is echoed in Proverbs 11:5, which states, "The righteousness of the blameless keeps his way straight, but the wicked falls by his own wickedness."

Conclusion: A Paradigm of Faithfulness Versus Apostasy

The Teacher of Righteousness and the Wicked Priest represent two opposing paradigms within the Dead Sea Scrolls: faithfulness to God's covenant versus outright apostasy. Their conflict encapsulates the struggle between righteousness and corruption, light and darkness, and covenantal loyalty versus betrayal. Through this narrative, the Qumran community reinforced the principles of purity, obedience, and the consequences of deviating from God's laws. The vindication of the Teacher of Righteousness and the anticipated judgment upon the Wicked Priest provided them with a profound assurance in the justice of Jehovah, who remains faithful to those who seek His ways and punishes those who forsake them.

Bibliography

Andrews, E. D. (2024). *THE DEAD SEA SCROLLS: What Is the Truth About the Dead Sea Scrolls?* Cambridge, OH: Christian Publishing House.

Boccaccini, G. (1998). *Beyond the Essene Hypothesis: The Parting of the Ways between Qumran and Enochic Judaism.* Grand Rapids, MI: Eerdmans.

Charlesworth, J. H. (Ed.). (1994). *The Dead Sea Scrolls: Hebrew, Aramaic, and Greek Texts with English Translations.* Tubingen: Mohr Siebeck.

Collins, J. J. (2019). *Apocalypticism in the Dead Sea Scrolls.* London: Routledge.

Davies, P. R., & Brooke, G. J. (1994). *Qumran and the History of the Biblical Text.* London: T&T Clark.

Eisenman, R. H., & Wise, M. (1992). *The Dead Sea Scrolls Uncovered: The First Complete Translation and Interpretation of 50 Key Documents.* Shaftesbury, Dorset: Element Books.

Evans, C. A., & Flint, P. W. (Eds.). (1999). *Eschatology, Messianism, and the Dead Sea Scrolls.* Grand Rapids, MI: Eerdmans.

Garcia Martinez, F., & Tigchelaar, E. (2000). *The Dead Sea Scrolls Study Edition.* Leiden: Brill.

H. Lim, T., & et al. (2004). *The Dead Sea Scrolls in Their Historical Context.* London; New York: T&T Clark.

Lim, T. H. (2005). *The Dead Sea Scrolls: A Very Short Introduction.* Oxford: Oxford University Press.

Schiffman, L. H. (1994). *Reclaiming the Dead Sea Scrolls: Their True Meaning for Judaism and Christianity.* Philadelphia, PA: Jewish Publication Society.

Tov, E. (2001). *Textual Criticism of the Hebrew Bible.* Minneapolis, MN: Fortress Press.

Edward D. Andrews

VanderKam, J. C. (2010). *The Dead Sea Scrolls Today*. Grand Rapids, MI:
Eerdmans.